# Pleasures

## PURE & SIMPLE
### & good for you, too!

## Brita Housez

FRONT COVER

*Grilled Marinated Salmon Steaks,* page 129

*Mesclun, Peach and Feta Salad,* page 67

# Pleasures: Pure & Simple
## by
## Brita Housez

**First Printing – September 2006**

**Library and Archives Canada Cataloguing in Publication**

Housez, Brita

Pleasures pure & simple : & good for you, too! / Brita Housez.

Includes index.
ISBN 10: 1-897010-35-4
ISBN 13: 978-1-897010-35-8

1. Cookery.  2. Entertaining.  I. Title.
TX714.H682  2006          641.5          C2006-904940-8


Photography by:
Patricia Holdsworth
Patricia Holdsworth Photography, Regina, Saskatchewan

Page and Cover Design by:
Brian Danchuk
Brian Danchuk Design, Regina, Saskatchewan

Page Formatting and Index by Iona Glabus
Centax Books


Designed, Printed and Produced in Canada by:
Centax Books, a Division of PrintWest Communications Ltd.
Publishing Director, Photo Designer & Food Stylist: Margo Embury
1150 Eighth Avenue, Regina, Saskatchewan, Canada  S4R 1C9
(306) 525-2304    FAX (306) 757-2439
E-mail: centax@printwest.com          www.centaxbooks.com

# Table of Contents

*Recipes have been tested in U.S. Standard measurements. Common metric measurements are given as a convenience for those who are more familiar with metric. Recipes have not been tested in metric.*

# Introduction

For most of us, eating good food constitutes one of life's simple pleasures. We tend to associate certain flavors and aromas with sensations and moods we experience while engaging in favorite activities and celebrations. You can probably relate to the appeal of a thick, juicy hamburger with all the trimmings after a long walk through the colorful autumn woods; the aroma and bursting good flavor of a freshly picked tomato still warm from the sun; a melt-in-your-mouth chocolate brownie whether you're feeling blue or on top of the world; a traditional Thanksgiving turkey dinner shared with family and friends. Who can forget the sensual pleasure conveyed by Albert Finney in the classic scene from the movie *Tom Jones* in which he hungrily gnaws on a chicken leg and other delicacies while suggestively gazing at Susannah York?

It is fair to say that I love to cook – provided I don't have to spend hours preparing a meal. Whether we are constrained by a busy schedule of work and/or family responsibilities or we have ample leisure time to enjoy the kitchen experience in a relaxed frame of mind, it is rewarding to produce good food with a minimum of fuss. For this book, I had fun creating new recipes as well as experimenting with old favorites which I simplified by using fewer ingredients and shorter, more efficient preparation – without sacrificing flavor and quality. I have attempted to bring together an eclectic collection of recipes, many of which enjoy a sprinkling of ethnic flavors.

In my previous cookbooks, *Tofu Mania* and *The Soy Dessert and Baking Book*, the theme was healthy cooking without sacrificing flavor. In the former, this was largely accomplished by including tofu as an ingredient in every recipe and by using it as a partial replacement for fats without compromising taste or texture. In the latter, the same strategy was applied specifically to desserts and baked goods using an array of soy products in addition to tofu.

While the focus in this book is not on healthy eating, health issues have remained important to me. Having made a conscious effort to cook "healthy" for most of my adult life, it was second nature for me to continue in this vein by incorporating lots of wholesome ingredients such as grains, nuts, seeds, legumes, vegetables and fruits into the recipes and by using reduced amounts of fat, most of it unsaturated. I use butter quite liberally in the desserts as I find it to be the best-tasting fat for sweets, especially pastries. I also use yogurt as a partial substitute for fats whenever it seems appropriate to do so.

With its many recipe variations and simple preparation instructions, *Pleasures* is an all-purpose cookbook which should satisfy most cooking needs for both experienced and novice cooks. My own cooking experience has led me to believe that pleasure very often starts in the kitchen.

Bon appetit!

*Brita Housez*

To all my family and friends

for whom I've had the pleasure of cooking.

## ACKNOWLEDGEMENTS

A big thank you to Margo Embury and Iona Glabus of Centax, Bev Jong, Brian Danchuk, Patricia Holdsworth, Chuck Laywine and all my "taste testers" for helping to make the cooking and writing process for this book a pleasurable experience.

*Pleasures*
PURE & SIMPLE

# BREAKFAST, BRUNCH & LUNCH

# FRESH FRUIT WITH MAPLE YOGURT

*A light breakfast, snack or dessert. Refreshingly pure and simple.*

| | |
|---|---|
| 1 cup / 250 mL | plain yogurt |
| 2 tbsp / 30 mL | maple syrup, or to taste |
| 2 cups / 500 mL | chopped fresh fruit and/or berries |
| 2 tbsp / 30 mL | shredded coconut, toasted (optional) |

In a medium bowl, stir together yogurt and maple syrup. Fold in fruit. Sprinkle with coconut, if desired.

Makes 4 to 5 servings

Pictured on page 17.

# STRAWBERRY AND PEACH BUTTERMILK SMOOTHIE

*Tasty, nourishing and healthy.*

| | |
|---|---|
| 1 cup / 250 mL | strawberries, rinsed and hulled |
| 2-3 | ripe peaches, peeled, pitted and quartered |
| 1 cup / 250 mL | buttermilk OR plain yogurt |
| 2-3 tbsp / 30-45 mL | liquid honey (depending on tartness of fruit) |
| 24 | ice cubes (optional) |

Combine all ingredients in a blender. Process until smooth.

Makes 2 servings

**Variations:** *Substitute your favorite seasonal fruit for the strawberries and peaches. Try oranges and bananas, mangoes and blueberries, raspberries and kiwis – use your tastebuds and your imagination.*

Pictured on page 17.

*Store maple syrup in the refrigerator after opening. This uniquely North American product is prized around the world for its rich, mellow flavor. Other fabulous maple treats are maple honey, maple butter and maple sugar.*

# BREAKFAST MUESLI

*This creamy-textured, great-tasting cold cereal is loaded with healthy nutrients and fiber. The oats and flaxseeds need to be soaked but the actual preparation time is minimal. A wholesome and energizing breakfast.*

| | |
|---|---|
| 1 tbsp / 15 mL | flaxseeds |
| 3 tbsp / 45 mL | water |
| 1 cup / 250 mL | large flaked oats |
| 2 tbsp / 30 mL | EACH, raisins and dried cranberries |
| | juice of 1 orange |
| | juice of 1 lemon |
| 1 | apple |
| ½ cup / 125 mL | plain yogurt |
| 3-4 tbsp / 45-60 mL | maple syrup |
| | berries for garnish (optional) |

Place flaxseeds in a small bowl and pour water over them. Cover and let soak 2 hours to overnight.

In a medium bowl, stir oats, raisins and cranberries with orange and lemon juices. Cover and chill 2 hours to overnight.

Shortly before serving, peel, core and shred apple. Fold apple, yogurt, maple syrup and flaxseeds into oat mixture. Garnish with berries, if desired.

Makes 4 to 6 servings

# BUCKWHEAT CRÊPES

*Buckwheat's nutritional properties and great flavor combine to make it a valuable addition to recipes like crêpes, pancakes, muffins and breads. Gluten-free buckwheat is rich in protein, antioxidants and fiber. Try these delicious crêpes with either a sweet or savory filling. At home, we enjoy them simply rolled up with a little jam or maple syrup.*

| | |
|---|---|
| 3 | eggs |
| 2 cups / 500 mL | milk |
| 1 cup / 250 mL | water |
| 2 tbsp / 30 mL | vegetable oil |
| 1 cup / 250 mL | unbleached flour |
| 1 cup / 250 mL | buckwheat flour |
| ¼ tsp / 1 mL | salt |

In a large bowl, using a fork, beat together eggs, milk and water. Beat in remaining ingredients until batter is smooth.

Heat a lightly greased frying pan over medium-high heat. Pour in enough batter to thinly coat bottom of pan. Tilt the pan in a circular motion to spread the batter thinly and evenly. Cook 30 to 40 seconds per side. Grease pan before frying remaining crêpes.

Stack crêpes on a plate. Serve immediately or cover with plastic wrap and refrigerate until ready to use, up to 2 days. Reheat in microwave oven.

Makes about 20, 8" (20 cm) crêpes

*Light buckwheat flour contains fewer hulls and is milder-tasting than the fiber-rich dark buckwheat flour. The famous Russian Blini, served with caviar, are made with buckwheat flour.*

# BUTTERMILK APPLE PANCAKES

*Who says healthy food can't be delicious? These low-fat pancakes taste every bit as good as the original recipe but the addition of soy protein powder, known for its many health benefits, makes them better for you. I like to enhance any recipe that calls for flour by replacing a couple of tablespoons of the flour with this protein-rich powder. No one has ever noticed!*

| | |
|---|---|
| 1 cup / 250 mL | unbleached flour |
| 2 tbsp / 30 mL | soy protein isolate powder |
| 1 tsp / 5 mL | baking powder |
| 1 tbsp / 15 mL | granulated sugar |
| 1 | egg, beaten |
| 1 cup / 250 mL | buttermilk |
| 2 | large apples, peeled, cored and shredded |
| | sugar and cinnamon for sprinkling |

In a medium bowl, combine flour, soy protein powder, baking powder and sugar. Stir in egg and buttermilk to form a smooth thick batter. Fold in apples.

Heat a large greased frying pan over medium heat. Drop 2 tbsp (30 mL) of batter per pancake into the hot pan, shaping them with the back of a fork so that each is about 2½" (6.5 cm) in diameter. Fry 2 to 3 minutes per side, or until lightly browned and cooked through. Grease pan before frying the next batch.

Transfer to a platter and sprinkle with sugar and cinnamon or serve with maple syrup.

Makes about 16 small pancakes

**Variations:** *Other chopped or grated fruit works well, too, e.g., pears, mangoes, nectarines, peaches, etc. If using juicy berries, the amount of liquid should be reduced.*

*Soy protein isolate is the purest form of soy protein, containing nearly all the essential amino acids necessary for good health. Low in fat and cholesterol, it is a valuable addition to breads, cereals, shakes, sauces, soups and infant formulas.*

# CORN PANCAKES

*Fresh corn, green onions and cilantro give these savory pancakes lots of flavor. A great brunch or side dish with grilled fish or meat.*

| | |
|---|---|
| ½ cup / 125 mL | unbleached flour |
| ¼ cup / 60 mL | corn flour |
| generous pinch | EACH, salt and pepper |
| ¼ tsp / 1 mL | baking powder |
| ¾ cup / 175 mL | plain yogurt |
| 2 | eggs, beaten |
| 2 | green onions, thinly sliced |
| 1 tbsp / 15 mL | chopped fresh cilantro |
| 1 cup / 250 mL | fresh or frozen corn kernels |

Combine flours, salt, pepper and baking powder in a medium bowl. Using a fork, mix in yogurt and eggs to form a thick smooth batter. Fold in onions, cilantro and corn.

Heat a large, lightly greased frying pan over medium heat. Drop 2 tbsp (30 mL) of batter per pancake into the hot pan, shaping each with the back of a fork into a 3" (7.5 cm) circle, ½" (1 cm) thick. Fry 3 to 4 minutes per side, or until lightly browned and cooked through. Grease pan before frying the next batch.

Corn pancakes can be made ahead and reheated in a microwave oven just before serving.

Makes about 12 small pancakes

# PEPPERONI AND CHEESE PIZZA FRITTATA

*A hearty lunch rich in protein, low in carbohydrates. Tasty, too.*

| | |
|---|---|
| 4 | eggs |
| 2 tbsp / 30 mL | water |
| 2 tbsp / 30 mL | milk |
| | salt and pepper, to taste |
| 2 tsp / 10 mL | vegetable oil |
| 3-4 tbsp / 45-60 mL | pizza sauce |
| generous pinch | EACH, dried parsley and oregano |
| 2 | green onions, thinly sliced |
| | sliced pepperoni OR chopped ham, chicken OR tofu |
| ½ cup / 125 mL | shredded Cheddar and mozzarella cheese, mixed |

In a medium bowl, whisk together eggs, water, milk, salt and pepper.

In a large frying pan, heat oil over medium-high heat. Pour egg mixture into pan and cook about 2 minutes, until it begins to set. Spoon pizza sauce over frittata and sprinkle with parsley, oregano and onions. Scatter pepperoni evenly over frittata and top with cheese. Reduce heat to low, cover and cook just long enough for cheese to melt, 2 to 3 minutes. Cut into wedges.

Makes 2 to 3 servings

*Variation*: *If your frying pan is ovenproof, place the cheese-topped frittata under a preheated broiler just until cheese is melted and pepperoni is heated through. This also works well to set the top of an omelet before folding – especially useful if you don't like omelets with a runny center.*

■■■ *Good news if you love eggs – the Harvard School of Public Health study found no significant link between eating eggs and developing cardiovascular disease. Eggs contain no trans fats, and they do not have a negative effect on blood cholesterol levels.*

# HASH-BROWN FRITTATA

*Very simple to make, especially if you have some leftover hash browns from yesterday's breakfast or dinner. You can throw in some vegetables, too, as well as some chopped ham or sausage. The variations are endless, so be creative!*

| | |
|---|---|
| 1 tbsp / 15 mL | vegetable oil |
| ½ | medium onion, chopped |
| 3-4 | mushrooms, sliced |
| ½ | red bell pepper, chopped |
| 1 cup / 250 mL | hash-brown potatoes |
| generous pinch | EACH, dried parsley and basil |
| | salt and pepper, to taste |
| 3 | eggs, beaten |
| ½ cup / 125 mL | shredded Cheddar cheese |

In a medium frying pan, heat oil over medium heat. Add onions, mushrooms and peppers and stir-fry about 5 minutes, or until lightly browned. Stir in potatoes and seasonings and cook until heated through.

Gently pour eggs over potatoes. Sprinkle with cheese. Reduce heat to low, cover and continue to cook about 5 minutes, or until eggs have set and cheese has melted. Cut into wedges and serve with your favorite salsa or chutney.

Makes 2 to 3 servings

*Eggs are an excellent source of high-quality protein, plus they contain significant amounts of several vitamins and minerals. Egg yolks contain lutein and zeaxanthin, antioxidants which help keep eyes healthy and decrease the risk of cataracts.*

# SPINACH AND ONION FRITTATA

*This protein and iron-rich light meal is suitable for dieters and people on the go.*

| | |
|---|---|
| 10 oz / 284 g | pkg spinach, fresh or frozen |
| 2 tsp / 10 mL | vegetable oil |
| ½ | medium onion, chopped |
| | salt and pepper, to taste |
| 3 | eggs, beaten |
| ½ cup / 125 mL | grated Cheddar OR Swiss cheese |

If using fresh spinach, cook it in ½ cup (125 mL) boiling water for 5 minutes. Drain and squeeze out excess moisture. If using frozen, thaw spinach. Squeeze out moisture.

In a medium frying pan, heat oil over medium heat. Add onion and sauté until translucent and starting to brown. Add spinach, spreading it evenly in pan. Sprinkle with salt and pepper. Pour eggs over spinach. Top with cheese. Cover, reduce heat to low and cook 5 minutes, or until eggs have set. Cut into wedges and serve with salsa, if desired.

Makes 2 to 3 servings

# SCRAMBLED EGGS WITH HAM AND CILANTRO

*A light nutritious snack, any time of day.*

| | |
|---|---|
| 8 | eggs |
| 2 tbsp / 30 mL | milk |
| 1 tsp / 5 mL | Dijon mustard |
| | salt and pepper, to taste |
| 2 tsp / 10 mL | vegetable oil |
| 4 | slices of ham |
| 1-2 tbsp / 15-30 mL | chopped cilantro |

In a medium bowl, whisk together eggs, milk, mustard, salt and pepper.

In a large frying pan, heat oil over medium heat. Add egg mixture and, using a spatula, push egg mixture back and forth to form large curds. When almost set, fold in ham and cilantro.

Makes 4 servings

# BLACK BEAN PUMPKIN SOUP

*A hearty soup, low in fat yet loaded with flavor.*

| | |
|---|---|
| 2, 19 oz / 540 mL | cans black beans, rinsed and drained |
| 19 oz / 540 mL | can stewed tomatoes |
| 2 tbsp / 30 mL | vegetable oil |
| 1 | large onion, chopped |
| 4-6 | garlic cloves, minced |
| 2 tsp / 10 mL | ground cumin |
| generous pinch | EACH, allspice, coriander and turmeric |
| | salt and pepper, to taste |
| 3 cups / 750 mL | chicken OR vegetable broth |
| 2 tbsp / 30 mL | granulated sugar |
| 19 oz / 540 mL | can pumpkin purée |
| ¼ cup / 60 mL | dry sherry OR apple juice |

In a food processor, or using a hand blender, coarsely purée beans with stewed tomatoes.

In a large saucepan, heat oil over high heat. Add onion and sauté 3 to 4 minutes, until starting to brown. Add garlic, cumin, allspice, coriander, turmeric, salt and pepper. Fold in bean and tomato purée. Stir in broth, sugar and pumpkin. Reduce heat to low and simmer, uncovered, about 20 minutes, stirring occasionally. Add sherry and continue to simmer 5 to 10 minutes, or until soup reaches the desired consistency. Adjust seasonings.

Makes about 7 cups (1.75 L)

## BRUNCH

# HARVEST VEGETABLE SOUP

*"Elegant comfort food" is what I call this creamy-textured, richly flavored soup. Serve it as a first course for Thanksgiving dinner or simply share it with your family as a main dish with the Buttermilk and Flaxseed Biscuits, page 33. Nutritious, yet light and almost fat-free.*

| | |
|---|---|
| 2 cups / 500 mL | vegetable OR chicken broth |
| 2 cups / 500 mL | diced squash |
| 1 cup / 250 mL | diced carrots |
| 1 cup / 250 mL | diced sweet potatoes OR parsnips |
| 1 | fennel bulb, diced (about 2 cups/500 mL) |
| 1 | medium onion, chopped |
| 1 | apple, chopped |
| 1 tsp / 5 mL | grated fresh ginger |
| generous pinch | EACH, cayenne pepper, dried tarragon and allspice |
| 1 cup / 250 mL | plain yogurt |
| several drops | Maggi Seasoning |

In a large saucepan over high heat, bring broth to a boil. Add vegetables, apple, ginger and spices. Return to a boil. Reduce heat to low, cover and simmer 20 minutes, or until vegetables are soft.

Using a food processor or blender, purée vegetable mixture until smooth. Blend in yogurt and Maggi Seasoning. If soup is too thick, add a little broth or water. Adjust seasonings and heat through. To serve, garnish with Herbed Croûtons, page 85, if desired.

Makes 6 servings

*Tips: To minimize preparation time, dice or chop vegetables in a food processor. This soup can be made ahead and reheated.*

# LATE-SUMMER GAZPACHO

*Make this full-bodied cold soup when sun-ripened, local tomatoes taste best and cost the least. Truly refreshing and surprisingly satisfying.*

| | |
|---|---|
| 6 | large tomatoes |
| 1 | cucumber, peeled |
| 1 | red OR green bell pepper |
| 1 | large onion |
| 2-3 | garlic cloves |
| small handful | fresh parsley OR cilantro |
| ¼ cup / 60 mL | red wine vinegar |
| ¼ cup / 60 mL | olive oil |
| 1½ tsp / 7 mL | salt, or to taste |
| several drops | Tabasco sauce |

Coarsely chop vegetables. Combine with remaining ingredients. Blend in a blender or food processor in 2 or 3 batches, leaving the gazpacho slightly chunky. Adjust seasonings.

Makes about 6 servings

*Variations*: Add a splash of Worcestershire sauce to taste. Top each bowl of soup with Herbed Croûtons, page 85.

# GREEN PEA, LEEK AND BACON SOUP

*A supremely easy soup with a lovely color and flavor.*

| | |
|---|---|
| 3-4 | slices of bacon, chopped |
| 2 | medium leeks, trimmed of dark green parts, chopped |
| 1 lb / 250 g | bag frozen sweet peas |
| 3 cups / 750 mL | chicken OR vegetable stock |
| ½ cup / 125 mL | half and half cream |

## GREEN PEA, LEEK AND BACON SOUP (CONTINUED)

In a deep saucepan, over high heat, fry bacon until crisp.

Add leeks and sauté 5 minutes. Add peas and chicken stock and bring to a boil. Reduce heat to low, cover and simmer 5 minutes, or until vegetables are soft. Remove from heat.

Blend mixture with a hand blender until fairly smooth. Blend in cream. Heat through and serve.

Makes 4 to 5 servings

## LEEK AND POTATO SOUP

*Simple, wholesome and delicious. Fresh herbs and lemon make this potato soup truly distinctive.*

| | |
|---|---|
| 4 cups / 1 L | chicken, beef OR vegetable broth, divided |
| 3 | large leeks, trimmed of dark green parts, chopped |
| 3 | medium potatoes, peeled and chopped |
| 1/2 cup / 125 mL | chopped ham |
| 2 tbsp / 30 mL | tomato paste |
| 1/4 cup / 60 mL | chopped fresh cilantro OR lovage |
| generous pinch | EACH, ground fennel and celery seed |
| | salt and pepper, to taste |
| 1 tbsp / 15 mL | lemon juice |

In a large saucepan, over high heat, bring 1 cup (250 mL) broth to a boil. Add remaining ingredients. Cover, reduce heat to low and simmer 10 to 15 minutes, or until vegetables are soft. Remove from heat.

Blend soup with a hand blender to a chunky consistency. Add remaining broth; return to a boil. Adjust seasonings and serve with a crusty grain bread such as Oat, Bulgar and Quinoa Bread, page 38.

Makes 4 to 6 servings

* Lovage has an intense celery flavor. It is also called maggi and "love parsley."

# COUNTRY-STYLE LENTIL SOUP

*Nutritious, flavorful and satisfying.*

| | |
|---|---|
| 2-3 | slices of bacon, chopped |
| 4 | medium carrots, finely chopped |
| 2-3 | stalks of celery, finely chopped |
| 2 | leeks, trimmed of dark green parts, sliced crosswise |
| 3-4 | garlic cloves, minced |
| 2, 14 oz / 398 mL | cans lentils, rinsed and drained |
| generous pinch | EACH, dried thyme, celery seeds and cumin salt and pepper, to taste |
| 19 oz / 540 mL | can stewed tomatoes |
| 4 cups / 1 L | chicken OR vegetable broth |
| 2 tbsp / 30 mL | chopped fresh parsley |

In a large saucepan, over high heat, fry bacon for 2 minutes.

Add carrots, celery, leeks and garlic and stir-fry until leeks have wilted. Stir in lentils; sprinkle with seasonings. Add stewed tomatoes and broth. Bring to a boil, cover and reduce heat to low. Simmer about 45 minutes.

Sprinkle individual servings with parsley.

Makes 6 servings

*Pictured on page 69.*

# BEAN AND BARLEY SOUP

*A "stick-to-the-ribs" kind of soup that tempts the palate with its savory aroma.*

| | |
|---|---|
| 1 tbsp / 15 mL | vegetable oil |
| 1 | medium onion, chopped |
| ½ cup / 125 mL | pearl barley |
| 4 cups / 1 L | chicken OR vegetable broth |
| ¼ cup / 60 mL | tomato paste |
| generous pinch | EACH, ground coriander, cumin and fennel seed salt and pepper, to taste |
| ½ cup / 125 mL | chopped leftover chicken OR other meat (optional) |
| 19 oz / 540 mL | can white OR kidney beans, rinsed and drained |
| 2 tbsp / 30 mL | chopped fresh parsley |

# BEAN AND BARLEY SOUP (CONTINUED)

In a medium saucepan, heat oil over medium heat. Add onion and barley and sauté for 2 minutes. Add broth. Stir in tomato paste, seasonings and chicken, if using. Bring to a boil, cover and reduce heat to low. Simmer for about 1 hour, or until barley is tender.

Add beans. If soup is too thick, add a little broth. Stir in parsley and cook until beans are heated through.

Makes 4 to 6 servings

# CORN AND POTATO CHOWDER

*I make this hearty chowder in September when corn is plentiful and evenings are getting cool.*

| | |
|---|---|
| 2 tbsp / 30 mL | butter OR vegetable oil |
| 1 | medium onion, diced |
| 1 | red bell pepper, seeded and diced |
| 3 | medium potatoes, peeled and cut into ½"/1 cm cubes |
| 2 cups / 500 mL | milk |
| 2 cups / 500 mL | vegetable broth |
| generous pinch | EACH, dried basil, thyme and coriander |
| | salt and pepper, to taste |
| 4 ears | corn, kernels removed, OR 2 cups/500 mL frozen |
| 1 tbsp /15 mL | chopped fresh cilantro |

In a large pot, melt butter over medium heat. Add onion and red pepper and stir-fry 3 to 5 minutes, or until onion is translucent. Add potatoes, milk, broth, basil, thyme, coriander, salt and pepper. Bring to a boil. Cover, reduce heat to low and simmer about 10 minutes. Stir in corn and simmer 4 minutes longer, or until vegetables are tender.

Transfer 2 cups (500 mL) of the solids to a blender and purée until smooth. Return to the pot. Adjust seasonings. Stir in cilantro and bring to a boil for 1 minute. If chowder is too thick, add a little milk or broth.

Makes 4 to 6 servings

# KASHA AND POTATO SOUP

*Wholesome goodness and a hint of Middle Eastern and Indian flavors make this soup popular in my house. My partner Chuck, who is generally not a soup enthusiast, enjoys this full-bodied soup whenever I make it.*

| | |
|---|---|
| 2 tbsp / 30 mL | vegetable oil |
| 1 | medium onion, finely chopped |
| 4 cups / 1 L | chicken, beef OR vegetable broth |
| 1 | large potato, chopped |
| ¼ cup / 60 mL | kasha (buckwheat groats) |
| 2 | medium tomatoes, skinned and chopped |
| ¼ cup / 60 mL | tomato paste |
| 2 tbsp / 30 mL | fresh lemon juice |
| generous pinch | EACH, cumin, coriander, dried oregano and basil |
| | salt, to taste |
| | cayenne pepper, to taste |
| 2 tbsp / 30 mL | chopped fresh cilantro |

In a medium saucepan, heat oil over medium heat. Add onion and stir-fry 2 to 3 minutes, until translucent. Add remaining ingredients. Reduce heat to low, cover and simmer 20 to 25 minutes, or until potatoes and kasha are tender. Add cilantro and cook another 5 minutes.

Makes 4 to 6 servings

*Buckwheat kasha is gluten-free. Kasha, in North America, refers to roasted buckwheat groats (kernels). Roasting gives the kernels a distinctive nutty flavor. Kasha is available in whole, coarse, medium and fine granulation and can be boiled, baked, steamed and served as a cereal or side dish, or added to soups and stews. It is a very good source of protein and is high in magnesium, phosphorus, potassium, vitamin B$_6$ and also a source of fiber, iron and zinc.*

# PANINI SANDWICHES

*Not long ago, I invested in a panini sandwich maker. It was money well spent as I've used it to make a variety of tasty sandwiches during the hot summer months. Its large surface, which can accommodate sandwiches of all shapes and sizes, makes it more versatile than a regular sandwich maker.*

Following are two recipes for scrumptious sandwiches.

# BRIE AND TOMATO SALSA PANINI SANDWICH

*Creamy, mellow Brie is fabulous with this zesty salsa.*

**Tomato Salsa:**

| | |
|---|---|
| 1 tsp / 5 mL | granulated sugar |
| | salt and pepper, to taste |
| 2 tbsp / 30 mL | balsamic vinegar |
| 2 tbsp / 30 mL | olive oil, divided |
| 2 | medium ripe tomatoes, chopped |
| 1 | medium sweet onion (e.g., Vidalia), chopped |
| 1 | yellow OR orange bell pepper, diced |
| 8-10 | fresh basil leaves, shredded |
| | |
| 8 | slices multi-grain bread |
| | Brie cheese, sliced (enough to fill 4 sandwiches) |

*To make the salsa*, In a medium bowl, stir together sugar, salt, pepper, vinegar and 1 tbsp (15 mL) oil. Fold in tomatoes, onion, bell pepper and basil.

Brush outside of bread slices with remaining oil. Divide Brie among 4 bread slices. Spread salsa over Brie. Top with remaining bread slices and press down gently.

Brown sandwiches in panini maker or fry them in a frying pan over medium heat, browning both sides.

Makes 4 sandwiches

*Pictured on page 69.*

# PANINI WESTERN SANDWICH

*This version of the classic Western or Denver sandwich is likely to become addictive.*

**Per Sandwich:**

| | |
|---|---|
| 2 | eggs |
| 2 tbsp / 30 mL | chopped green onion |
| ½ tsp / 2 mL | minced chili pepper (optional) |
| 1-2 | slices of ham |
| | salt and pepper, to taste |
| 2 | slices bread OR 1 panini OR Kaiser roll |
| 2 tsp / 10 mL | olive oil |
| small handful | baby spinach |
| ¼ cup / 60 mL | grated Cheddar OR Swiss cheese |

In a small bowl, whisk together eggs, onion, chili pepper (if using), ham, salt and pepper.

In a frying pan, heat oil over medium heat. Add egg mixture and cook, covered, 4 to 5 minutes, or until top is set and underside is lightly browned.

Brush outside of bread slices with a little oil.

Cut omelette to fit the bottom bread slice. Top with spinach leaves and cheese. Cover with remaining bread slice.

Brown sandwich in panini maker or fry sandwich in a frying pan over medium heat, browning both sides.

Makes 1 sandwich

# CHICKEN, CORN AND TOMATO QUESADILLAS

*Grilled or pan-fried, these quesadillas always hit the spot. Simple ingredients, lots of flavor.*

| | |
|---|---|
| ³/₄-1 lb / 375-500 g | skinless boneless chicken breasts |
| | salt and pepper, to taste |
| 2 tbsp / 30 mL | vegetable oil |
| 2 | garlic cloves, crushed |
| ½ cup / 125 mL | cooked corn kernels |
| ½ cup / 125 mL | chopped ripe tomatoes |
| 2 | green onions, thinly sliced |
| 1-2 tbsp / 15-30 mL | balsamic vinegar |
| 2 tbsp / 30 mL | vegetable oil, divided |
| 1 tsp / 5 mL | granulated sugar |
| 4, 10" / 25 cm | tortillas |
| 2 tbsp / 30 mL | honey mustard |
| 2 tbsp / 30 mL | mayonnaise |
| ½ cup / 125 mL | shredded, loosely packed fresh basil leaves |
| 1 cup / 250 mL | shredded provolone OR Asiago cheese |

Slice chicken breasts into thin strips. Sprinkle with salt and pepper.

In a wok or frying pan, heat oil over high heat. Add chicken and stir-fry 4 to 5 minutes, or until lightly browned and cooked through. Fold in garlic and continue to cook 1 minute. Set aside.

In a medium bowl, combine corn, tomatoes, onions, vinegar, 1 tbsp (15 mL) oil, sugar, salt and pepper.

Place tortillas on a clean work surface. Spread half of each tortilla with mustard and the other half with mayonnaise, leaving a ½" (1 cm) border. Layer half of each tortilla with the chicken, corn and tomato mixture, basil leaves and cheese. Fold uncovered half over filling and press gently to close. Brush both sides with remaining 1 tbsp (15 mL) oil.

Grill or pan-fry quesadillas over medium heat for 2 to 4 minutes per side, or until filling is heated through and the surface is lightly browned.

Makes 4 servings

# GREEK TOMATO TART

*Intensify the delicate flavor of sun-ripened tomatoes by first roasting them in a slow oven, then baking them in a puff pastry shell. Pure pleasure!*

| | |
|---|---|
| 1 lb / 500 g | tomatoes, thickly sliced |
| 1 tbsp / 15 mL | olive oil |
| 1 tsp / 5 mL | granulated sugar |
| generous pinch | EACH, dried oregano, cilantro, salt and pepper |
| 2 | garlic cloves, minced |
| 10x10" / 25x25 cm | prerolled sheet frozen puff pastry, thawed but cold |
| 2 tbsp / 30 mL | sliced kalamata olives |
| 1-2 tbsp / 15-30 mL | crumbled feta cheese |
| 1 tbsp / 15 mL | bread crumbs |

Preheat oven to 325°F (160°C).

Place tomato slices in a single layer on a parchment-lined rimmed baking sheet. Drizzle with olive oil and sprinkle with sugar, oregano, cilantro, salt and pepper. Scatter garlic over top. Bake 1 hour 15 minutes. Let cool. Can be made a day ahead to this point.

Preheat oven to 350°F (180°C).

Place pastry on a parchment-lined baking sheet; prick with a fork.

Spread tomatoes over pastry, leaving a 1" (2.5 cm) border. Sprinkle with olives, feta and bread crumbs. Bake 25 to 30 minutes, or until pastry is puffed and golden. Serve immediately.

Makes 4 servings

# SWEET ONION GALETTE

*As far back as I can remember, my mother used to make this wonderful savory pie about twice a year. I love it today as much as I did then, and so does my family. Here is my version of her prize-winning recipe.*

**Pastry:**

| | |
|---|---|
| 2 cups / 500 mL | unbleached flour |
| 1 tsp / 5 mL | salt |
| ½ cup / 125 mL | olive oil |
| ½ cup / 125 mL | warm milk |

**Onion Filling:**

| | |
|---|---|
| 4-6 | slices bacon, chopped |
| 2-3 | large sweet onions (e.g., Vidalia) |
| 2 tsp / 10 mL | caraway seeds |
| generous pinch | EACH, ground fennel, coriander and dried basil |
| 2 tbsp / 30 mL | cornstarch |
| ¾ cup / 175 mL | sour cream |
| 1 | egg, beaten |
| | salt and pepper, to taste |

*To make the crust*, combine all pastry ingredients in a food processor or by hand in a medium bowl. Wrap in a ball, cover and refrigerate 15 minutes to overnight.

Preheat oven to 425°F (220°C).

In a large frying pan, cook bacon over medium heat for about 2 minutes. Add onions and sauté 5 minutes, or until starting to brown. Reduce heat to low and simmer 15 minutes, stirring occasionally. Remove from heat and let cool 5 minutes. Fold in remaining ingredients.

Roll out dough to fit a 12" (30 cm) pizza pan (edge of dough can be irregular). Spread filling over dough, leaving a 2½" (6 cm) border. Fold border over filling.

Bake for about 30 minutes, or until lightly browned. Serve warm or at room temperature.

Makes 6 generous servings

# VEGETARIAN PRESTO PIZZA

*Homemade "fresh out of the oven" good flavor, yet quick and very easy to make as most of the toppings are available, ready to assemble, at your favorite deli antipasto bar.*

|  |  |
|---|---|
|  | pizza dough for a 12"/30 cm crust, pages 31 and 32, OR store-bought |
| 1 tbsp / 15 mL | olive oil |
| ¼ cup / 60 mL | pizza sauce |
| ¼ cup / 60 mL | grated Parmesan cheese |
| ½ cup / 125 mL | raw baby spinach |
| ¼ cup / 60 mL | chopped onion |
| ¼ cup / 60 mL | sliced olives |
| ¼ cup / 60 mL | roasted red peppers, cut into thin strips |
| ¼ cup / 60 mL | sun-dried tomatoes in oil, drained, cut into thin strips |
| ½ cup / 125 mL | marinated artichoke hearts, drained, coarsely chopped |
| ½ cup / 125 mL | shredded mozzarella cheese |

Preheat oven to 425°F (220°C).

Roll out dough to fit pizza pan. Brush with olive oil. Leaving a 1" (2.5 cm) border, spread pizza sauce over dough and sprinkle with Parmesan. Layer remaining toppings in the order listed. Bake 15 minutes, or until cheese has melted and crust is lightly browned.

Makes 6 to 8 slices

*Variations:* **To grill on the barbecue**, *place rolled out pizza dough on a greased grill over medium-high heat for 5 minutes. Turn and grill another 5 minutes. Transfer to a baking sheet and layer toppings. Return to grill, close lid and cook 5 minutes, or until cheese has melted.*

*Add other toppings such as leftover chopped meat or seafood, if desired. Substitute feta cheese for mozzarella for a flavor variation.*

# TRADITIONAL PIZZA CRUST (WITH YEAST)

*Yeast gives pizza crust the wonderful crisp and doughy texture of freshly baked bread. It's easy to make but needs time to rise before it can be baked. The following recipe makes enough dough for two medium-sized pizzas. Half of the dough can be frozen for future use.*

| | |
|---|---|
| 2 tsp / 10 mL | cornmeal |
| 2 tsp / 10 mL | honey |
| 1 cup / 250 mL | warm water |
| 1 tbsp / 15 mL | active dry yeast (1 pkg) |
| 2-2½ cups / 500-625 mL | unbleached flour |
| 2 tsp / 10 mL | salt |
| ¼ cup / 60 mL | olive oil |

Lightly grease two 12" (30 cm) pizza pans. Sprinkle them with cornmeal.

In a small bowl, dissolve honey in warm water. Stir in yeast and let sit 10 minutes, or until bubbly.

In a medium bowl, mix flour, salt, yeast mixture and oil. Knead until smooth and elastic, about 5 minutes, then shape into a ball. Cover and let rise until doubled in bulk, 45 to 60 minutes.

Transfer dough to a floured work surface. Cut in half. Roll out and stretch dough to fit prepared pans. Cut off and discard any overlapping dough. Top with desired toppings and bake 15 minutes in a 425°F (220°C) oven.

Makes two 12" (30 cm) pizzas

# QUICK PIZZA CRUST (WITH BAKING POWDER)

*For a change, you may want to try this delicious biscuit-like crust which takes less time to prepare than traditional pizza crust made with yeast. Cornmeal adds flavor and texture.*

| | |
|---|---|
| 2 cups / 500 mL | unbleached flour |
| ¼ cup / 60 mL | cornmeal |
| 1½ tbsp / 22 mL | baking powder |
| 2 tsp / 10 mL | salt |
| ⅔ cup / 150 mL | milk |
| ⅓ cup / 75 mL | olive oil |

In a medium bowl, combine flour, cornmeal, baking powder and salt. Stir in milk and oil. Knead just until dough sticks together. Pat dough into a ball, cover and let rest 15 minutes.

Meanwhile, grease a 12" (30 cm) pizza pan.

Transfer dough to a floured work surface and cover with a sheet of waxed paper. Roll out dough to fit pan. Remove waxed paper. Top with desired toppings and bake 20 to 25 minutes at 400°F (200°C).

Makes one 12" (30 cm) pizza

*Variation: This crust is also easily adapted for a* **Fresh Fruit Pizza** *– substitute vegetable oil for the olive oil and add 1 tbsp. (15 mL) sugar. Reduce salt to 1 tsp (5 mL). Bake as above until firm and golden, 15 to 20 minutes. Glaze cooled crust with melted fruit jelly, top with sliced fresh fruit and glaze with the melted jelly.*

# BUTTERMILK AND FLAXSEED BISCUITS

*It's easy to get hooked on these delicious good-for-you biscuits. The nutty-flavored flaxseeds are heart-healthy and rich in cancer-preventing antioxidants, so feel free to add them to all your favorite dishes. Throw a handful into cookie, bread or pie dough and sprinkle some over cereal, pizza or salads. For easy digestion, grind flaxseeds or soak them in water before using them in a recipe.*

| | |
|---|---|
| 2 tbsp / 30 mL | flaxseeds |
| ¼ cup / 60 mL | water |
| 2½ cups / 625 mL | unbleached flour |
| 2 tbsp / 30 mL | baking powder |
| 1 tsp / 5 mL | salt |
| 6 tbsp / 90 mL | unsalted butter |
| 1 cup / 250 mL | buttermilk |

In a small bowl, combine flaxseeds with water. Cover and let soak 2 hours to overnight.

Preheat oven to 400°F (200°C).

In a medium bowl, combine flour, baking powder and salt. Mix in butter with a pastry blender until mixture is evenly crumbly. Stir in flaxseeds and buttermilk. Knead a few seconds on a lightly floured work surface until dough forms a soft ball. Roll or pat to ¾" (2 cm) thickness. Cut with a 2" (5 cm) cookie cutter and place rounds on a parchment-lined baking sheet 1" (2.5 cm) apart.

Bake 18 to 20 minutes. Serve warm.

Makes 12 to 14 biscuits

■■■ *Whole flaxseed may be stored at room temperature for up to 1 year. Breaking up the flaxseed provides the most nutritional benefit. You can grind flaxseed in a coffee grinder, food processor or blender. Store ground flaxseed in the refrigerator in an airtight, opaque container, or in the freezer, for up to 3 months. Note: Baked items containing a large percentage of ground flaxseed will brown more quickly.*

# POPOVERS

*These popovers should be popping right over the edge of their tins when you take them out of the oven. Enjoy them with your favorite jam while they are warm and puffed.*

| | |
|---|---|
| 3 | large eggs |
| 3/4 cup / 175 mL | milk |
| 1 tbsp / 15 mL | butter, melted |
| 1 cup / 250 mL | unbleached flour |
| 1/4 tsp / 1 mL | salt |

Preheat oven to 450°F (230°C).

Grease 8 large muffin tins.

Using a whisk or hand blender, mix together eggs, milk and butter. Add flour and salt and beat until smooth.

Fill muffin tins half full and bake 20 minutes. Reduce oven temperature to 350°F (175°C) and bake 10 minutes longer, or until puffed and lightly browned.

Makes 8 large popovers

*Variations: To make* **Parmesan Popovers**, *fill muffin tins ¼ full. Sprinkle 1 tbsp. (15 mL) Parmesan cheese over batter in each muffin tin. Top with remaining batter. Bake as above.*

*To make* **Yorkshire Pudding**, *reduce the milk by ¼ cup (60 mL). Fill greased muffin tins and gently spoon ½ tbsp (7 mL) of roast drippings over the batter in each muffin tin. Bake as above.*

# BLUEBERRY AND CORNMEAL MUFFINS

*A "must-try" recipe. It's that good!*

| | |
|---|---|
| ½ cup / 125 mL | butter, softened |
| 1 cup / 250 mL | granulated sugar |
| 2 | large eggs |
| ¼ cup / 60 mL | fresh lemon juice |
| | grated zest of 1 lemon |
| 1 cup / 250 mL | unbleached flour |
| 1 cup / 250 mL | cornmeal |
| 4 tsp / 20 mL | baking powder |
| pinch | salt |
| ½ cup / 125 mL | milk |
| 1½ cups / 375 mL | fresh blueberries* |

Preheat oven to 375°F (190°C).

Grease 12 regular muffin tins or line with paper cups.

In a medium bowl, cream butter and sugar together. Beat in eggs, lemon juice and zest. Gradually fold in flour, cornmeal, baking powder and salt until just combined. Stir in milk. Very gently fold blueberries into batter to prevent bruising and bleeding.

Spoon batter into tins. This amount of batter will fill muffin tins to the top. Bake about 25 minutes, or until toothpick inserted in center comes out clean. Let sit in tins for 10 minutes, then turn out onto a wire rack to cool.

Makes 12 muffins

* If using frozen berries, fold them into batter while still frozen. If thawed, they will bleed into the batter, causing it to turn a grayish blue color.

*Editor's Note: My daughter substituted ½ cup (125 mL) of fresh raspberries for ½ cup (125 mL) of the blueberries and the flavor was fabulous. They were so moist that they didn't rise as much as the regular recipe – but WOW!*

*Pictured on page 17.*

# BANANA ORANGE BREAD

*How often do you throw away overripe bananas because you don't know what else to do with them? Next time, use them to make this delicious orange-laced quick bread.*

| | |
|---|---|
| 4 | ripe bananas |
| | juice and grated zest of 1 orange |
| 1/2 cup / 125 mL | butter, softened |
| 3/4 cup / 175 mL | granulated sugar |
| 2 | eggs, beaten |
| 1 1/2 cups / 375 mL | unbleached flour |
| 1/2 cup / 125 mL | whole-wheat flour |
| 1 tbsp / 15 mL | baking powder |
| pinch | salt |
| 1/4 cup / 60 mL | chopped pecans (optional) |

Preheat oven to 350°F (180°C). Grease a 9 x 5 x 3" (23 x 13 x 8 cm) loaf pan or line with parchment paper.

Purée bananas in blender or mash with a fork. Fold in orange juice and zest.

In a large bowl, cream butter and sugar together. Mix in eggs, flours, baking powder and salt until just combined. Fold in banana mixture and pecans, if using. Pour batter into pan.

Bake about 1 hour 15 minutes, or until a toothpick inserted in center comes out clean. Let sit 10 minutes, then turn out onto a wire rack to cool.

Makes 1 loaf, about 16 slices

*Bananas are rich in potassium, magnesium and vitamin C. They are also low in fat and high in "good" carbs – making them an excellent energy source for athletes. Do not refrigerate green bananas, however, overripening can be delayed by refrigerating them once they are ripe. Or, freeze ripe bananas for use in smoothies or baking.*

# SWEET POTATO, CRANBERRY AND WALNUT QUICK BREAD

*Just stir all the ingredients together and bake. Simple, wholesome and delicious, with lovely color and texture.*

| | |
|---|---|
| 2 | eggs |
| 1/2 cup / 125 mL | granulated sugar |
| 1/3 cup / 75 mL | vegetable oil |
| 1 1/2 cups / 375 mL | shredded sweet potato |
| 1 cup / 250 mL | unbleached flour |
| 1/2 cup / 125 mL | whole-wheat flour |
| 1 tbsp / 15 mL | baking powder |
| generous pinch | EACH, ground cinnamon, ground cloves and salt |
| 1/4 cup / 60 mL | chopped walnuts |
| 1/4 cup / 60 mL | dried cranberries |

Preheat oven to 350°F (180°C). Grease a 9 x 5 x 3" (23 x 13 x 8 cm) loaf pan or line with parchment paper.

In a large bowl, whisk together eggs, sugar and oil. Mix in remaining ingredients to form a thick batter. Spoon into prepared pan.

Bake 50 minutes, or until toothpick inserted in center comes out clean. Let sit 10 minutes, then turn out onto a wire rack to cool.

Makes 1 loaf, about 16 slices

*Variation: Substitute pecans for walnuts if you prefer.*

# OAT, BULGAR AND QUINOA BREAD

*Yeast breads require rising time, so they take longer to make than quick breads (which use baking powder as the leavening agent). However, homebaked yeast breads are a special treat and they keep fresh for several days. In this wholesome recipe, I've included oats, bulgar and quinoa, but other grain cereals work just as well.*

| | |
|---|---|
| 1 cup / 250 mL | rolled oats |
| 1/4 cup / 60 mL | bulgar |
| 1/4 cup / 60 mL | quinoa kernels |
| 2 1/2 cups / 625 mL | boiling water |
| 2 tbsp / 30 mL | liquid honey, divided |
| 1/2 cup / 125 mL | warm water |
| 2 tbsp / 30 mL | active dry yeast (2 pkgs) |
| 3/4-1 tbsp / 12-15 mL | salt |
| 1 cup / 250 mL | grated firm tofu |
| 1/2 cup / 125 mL | whole-wheat flour |
| 4-4 1/2 cups / 1-1.125 kg | unbleached flour |
| 1/2 cup / 125 mL | chopped walnuts |

In a large bowl, combine oats, bulgar and quinoa. Pour boiling water over cereal, cover and let soak 20 minutes.

Meanwhile, in a small bowl, dissolve 1 tbsp (15 mL) honey in warm water. Add yeast and let stand 10 minutes, or until yeast is bubbly, then stir. Fold into cereal mixture along with salt, tofu and remaining 1 tbsp (15 mL) honey. Gradually blend in flours to make a firm but slightly moist dough. Mix in nuts. Knead in same bowl for about 5 minutes, adding a little warm water if dough is too dry. Gather dough into a ball; place in a greased bowl, turning to grease top. Cover; let rise in warm place, free from draft, until doubled in bulk, 1 to 1 1/2 hours.

Turn dough out onto a floured surface. Punch dough down. Cut dough in half and shape into 2 loaves. Place in greased 9 x 5 x 3" (23 x 13 x 8 cm) loaf pans; cover and let rise again until doubled in bulk, about 1 hour.

Bake at 400°F (200°C) for 30 to 35 minutes. Let rest 5 minutes. Remove loaves from pans and let cool on wire racks.

Makes 2 loaves, about 12 slices each

*Pleasures*
PURE & SIMPLE

# APPETIZERS
# &
# DRINKS

# SPICED NUTS

*These nuts rock! Terrific with beer, wine or any other drink.*

| | |
|---|---|
| 1 | egg white |
| 6 cups / 1.5 L | salted mixed nuts |
| 1 cup / 250 mL | granulated sugar |
| 1 tsp / 5 mL | EACH, curry powder, ground cumin, cayenne pepper and paprika |
| ½ tsp / 2 mL | EACH, cinnamon and allspice |

Preheat oven to 325°F (160°C). Line a large baking sheet with parchment paper.

In a large bowl, whisk egg white until foamy. Stir in nuts. Add remaining ingredients and stir well to coat. Spread nuts evenly on baking sheet.

Bake 25 to 30 minutes, until nuts are lightly browned, stirring twice to break them up. Place baking sheet on a wire rack and lift nuts with a spatula to loosen them. Let cool. Store in an airtight container until ready to serve, up to 2 weeks.

Makes about 8 cups (2.25 L)

**Variation**: *If you need or want to cut back on sugar, use ½ cup (125 mL) of sugar or omit sugar completely. The flavor is different, but still fantastic.*

*Pictured on page 51.*

*Even though nuts are high in fat, it is "good" fat – monounsaturated, which helps to reduce the levels of "bad" (LDL) cholesterol. Scientific studies have shown that 1 ounce of nuts per day can reduce the risk of heart disease by up to 10 percent. Almonds, walnuts, pecans, hazelnuts, Brazil nuts, pistachios and macadamia nuts are the highest in monounsaturated fat. With their high fat content, nuts tend to go rancid. Store fresh shelled nuts in an airtight container in the refrigerator for up to 4 months, or in the freezer for up to 6 months.*

# OAT AND WALNUT CRISPS

*Occasionally, it's a real treat to have homemade crackers. These savory crisps go well with either sweet or salty foods. Try them with cream cheese topped with a little cranberry sauce. They're also delicious with the Spinach, Feta and Walnut Dip, page 44.*

| | |
|---|---|
| 1 cup / 250 mL | unbleached flour |
| ½ cup / 125 mL | whole-wheat flour |
| 2 cups / 500 mL | large flaked oats |
| 1 cup / 250 mL | coarsely chopped walnuts |
| 2 tbsp / 30 mL | granulated sugar |
| 1½ tsp / 7 mL | baking soda |
| ³/₄ cup / 175 mL | unsalted butter |
| ½ cup / 125 mL | water |

Preheat oven to 325°F (160°C).

In a large bowl, combine dry ingredients. Cut in butter with a pastry cutter until mixture resembles coarse crumbs. Add water and shape dough into a ball. Cover and let rest 30 minutes.

Cut dough into 4 portions. On a floured surface, using a floured rolling pin, roll out each portion to about ¼" (6 mm) thickness. Using a 2" (5 cm) round cookie cutter, cut out crackers and place them on a parchment-lined baking sheet.

Bake 20 minutes, or until lightly browned. Serve warm. Reheat leftover crackers in regular oven to restore crispness.

Makes about 60 crackers

*Variation*: If you prefer, substitute pecans for walnuts.

# CHEDDAR AND SESAME CHIPS

*These well-seasoned chips are hard to resist. The first time I experimented with this recipe, I couldn't stop eating them. By the time the second batch of six chips came out of the oven, I had already polished off the first batch! Now that the rest of the family have sampled these yummy chips, I'm lucky if I can sneak a single one for myself!*

| | |
|---|---|
| 2 cups / 500 mL | loosely packed shredded Cheddar cheese |
| 2 tbsp / 30 mL | sesame seeds |
| 1 tbsp / 15 mL | unbleached OR whole-wheat flour |
| generous pinch | cayenne pepper |

Preheat oven to 350°F (180°C).

Toss all ingredients together in a medium bowl. Transfer mixture by the heaping tablespoonful (22 mL) to a parchment-lined baking sheet, leaving 2" (5 cm) between mounds.

Bake about 10 minutes, or until cheese has completely melted. Loosen rounds with a knife or spatula and drape over a paper-towel-lined rolling pin (to curl the chips and absorb the fat). Let cool completely. Serve as an appetizer or snack, or as an accompaniment to soups or salads. Best when served the same day.

Makes 12 to 14 large chips

*Pictured on page 51.*

# CREAMY HUMMUS

*Plain yogurt gives this zesty appetizer its creamy texture. Very little fat but simply loaded with flavor!*

| | |
|---|---|
| 14 oz / 398 mL | can garbanzo beans (chickpeas) |
| 3 | garlic cloves, peeled and crushed |
| | juice and grated zest of ½ lemon |
| 2 tbsp / 30 mL | plain yogurt |
| 1 tbsp / 15 mL | olive oil |
| 1 tbsp / 15 mL | soy sauce |
| ¼ tsp / 1 mL | EACH, ground fennel, cumin, allspice, coriander and dried basil |
| | pepper, to taste |

Rinse and drain chickpeas. Transfer to blender. Add remaining ingredients. Blend until smooth or leave slightly chunky, if desired. Adjust seasonings. Serve with fresh crusty bread or crackers.

Makes about 2 cups (500 mL)

*Variations: For an interesting flavor variation, use half black beans and half garbanzo beans, or substitute a can of assorted mixed beans for the garbanzo beans. You may also want to try a sprinkle of red pepper flakes for added zest.*

*Garbanzo beans have a crunchy texture and a mild, nutty flavor. They are a wonderful addition to soups, stews and salads. They are also an excellent source of folic acid, magnesium and of soluble fiber, which helps to lower cholesterol levels and stabilize blood sugar levels, a major benefit for diabetics or people with hypoglycemia. Garbanzo beans also provide iron and manganese and are a good source of protein. The earliest recorded use of garbanzo beans goes back about 7,000 years.*

# SPINACH, FETA AND WALNUT DIP

*Lately, this dip has become a favorite at our house. It's a real winner with both family and friends.*

| | |
|---|---|
| 10 oz / 285 g | pkg spinach, fresh or frozen |
| 1/3 cup / 75 mL | crumbled feta |
| 2 tbsp / 30 mL | sour cream |
| 2 tbsp / 30 mL | mayonnaise |
| 1/4 cup / 60 mL | chopped roasted walnuts |
| 1 | garlic clove, minced (optional) |

If using fresh spinach, cook it in 1/2 cup (125 mL) boiling water for 5 minutes. Drain and squeeze out excess moisture. If using frozen, thaw spinach. Squeeze out moisture.

Coarsely chop spinach.

In a medium bowl, combine all ingredients with a fork. Refrigerate until ready to serve, up to 3 days. Great with crackers or corn chips, or with the Oat and Walnut Crisps on page 41.

Makes about 1 cup (250 mL)

**Variations:** *Did you know that almonds are a fruit? Hence, many people with (tree) nut allergies can enjoy this flavorful dip by substituting chopped, roasted almonds for the walnuts.*

*Pictured on page 51.*

# CHIPOTLE AND FETA DIP

*Mildly spiced or fiery hot, it's up to you.*

| | |
|---|---|
| 5 oz / 140 g | feta cheese, softened |
| 4 oz / 115 g | cream cheese, softened |
| ½ cup / 125 mL | plain yogurt |
| 1 tbsp / 15 mL | chopped chipotle chiles*, more or less |
| 1 tbsp / 15 mL | snipped chives |

In a medium bowl, cream together feta and cream cheese. Fold in yogurt, chipotles and chives. Cover and refrigerate up to 1 day. Serve with tacos, chips and raw vegetables.

Makes about 2 cups (500 mL)

* Chipotle chile peppers are dried, smoked jalapeño peppers. They can be purchased dried, canned (in adobo sauce) or pickled.

# MANGO AND SPICY CHEDDAR SPREAD

*Hot and sweet, this is so simple and so seductive.*

| | |
|---|---|
| 8 oz / 250 g | cold-pack Cheddar cheese (Imperial Cheese) |
| 8 oz / 250 g | cream cheese (not spreadable) |
| 3-5 tbsp / 45-75 mL | curry powder, to taste |
| 1 tbsp / 15 mL | brandy OR cognac |
| | finely chopped hot OR sweet mango chutney for topping |

Combine cheeses, curry and brandy in a food processor and blend until smooth. Spread in a 9 or 10" (23 or 25 cm) quiche or pie plate. Refrigerate to set. Spread chutney over cheese mixture, cover and refrigerate up to 1 day. Serve with crackers.

Makes 12 to 15 servings

# GARLICKY SUN-DRIED TOMATO BAKED BRIE

*Buttery Brie with a zesty garlicky topping - a melt-in-your-mouth appetizer.*

| | |
|---|---|
| 1½-2 lb / 750 g-1 kg | Brie round |
| 1 cup / 250 mL | chopped sun-dried tomatoes, in oil |
| 6-8 | garlic cloves, minced |
| 3 tbsp / 45 mL | balsamic vinegar |
| 2 tbsp / 30 mL | chopped fresh basil or 2 tsp/10 mL dried |
| ¾-1 cup / 175-250 mL | chopped fresh parsley |
| ¼-½ tsp / 1-2 mL | red pepper flakes |
| | freshly ground black pepper, to taste |

Place Brie in a baking dish or quiche pan just large enough to hold it. Score top of Brie.

Combine remaining ingredients and spread evenly over Brie. (At this point, Brie may be covered with plastic wrap and refrigerated up to 24 hours.)

Bake Brie at 350°F (180°C) for 20 to 25 minutes (longer if it was refrigerated), until cheese is hot and runny. Serve with water biscuits or baguette slices.

Makes 20 to 30 servings

*Variations: For* **Garlicky Red Pepper Baked Brie**, *combine 2 finely chopped red peppers, 6 tbsp (90 mL) chopped fresh parsley or basil, 4 garlic cloves minced, 1 tbsp (15 mL) Dijon mustard, 3 tbsp (45 mL) balsamic vinegar, 2 tbsp (30 mL) olive oil and freshly ground black pepper to taste. Spread over Brie and bake as above.*

*For* **Chutney or Salsa Baked Brie**, *spread Apricot and Apple Chutney, page 92, OR Apple and Cranberry Salsa, page 91, over Brie and bake as above.*

# CAPONATA CROSTINI

*A panoply of sautéed fresh vegetables makes this Sicilian specialty a tasty crostini topping.*

| | |
|---|---|
| ¼ cup / 60 mL | olive oil |
| ½ | fennel bulb, chopped |
| 2 | small Italian eggplants, chopped |
| 1 | red bell pepper, chopped |
| 1 | yellow bell pepper, chopped |
| ½ | serrano pepper, minced (optional) |
| 4 | garlic cloves, minced |
| ¾ cup / 175 mL | tomato sauce |
| 3 tbsp / 45 mL | red wine vinegar |
| ¼ cup / 60 mL | pitted, sliced green OR kalamata olives |
| 2 tbsp / 30 mL | EACH, chopped Italian parsley and basil |
| 2 tsp / 10 mL | sugar |
| | salt, to taste |
| | |
| | baguette, sliced and toasted |
| | snipped chives |

In a large saucepan, heat oil over high heat. Add fennel, eggplant and peppers, stir-fry about 5 minutes, until starting to brown. Add garlic, tomato sauce and vinegar. Cover, reduce heat to low and simmer 10 to 15 minutes, stirring occasionally. Fold in olives, parsley, basil, sugar and salt. Continue to simmer, uncovered, until vegetables are tender and caponata has reached a soft, thick consistency. Adjust seasonings. Serve warm or at room temperature on toasted baguette slices; sprinkle with chives.

Makes 3 to 4 cups (750 mL to 1 L), enough to generously top 25 to 30 crostini

*Tip: To minimize preparation time, coarsely chop vegetables in a food processor.*

# MINI TORTILLA CANAPÉS

*These little corn tortillas, topped with refried beans, tomatoes and cheese, look and taste terrific. You may want to try other toppings, such as guacamole or chopped spicy chorizo sausage with tomato salsa. I sometimes keep a batch of these crisp minis in my freezer, ready to assemble for unexpected guests.*

**Corn Tortillas:**

| | |
|---|---|
| 1 cup / 250 mL | cornmeal |
| 1 cup / 250 mL | unbleached flour |
| ¼ cup / 60 mL | olive oil |
| ½ cup / 125 mL | water |
| pinch | salt |

**Toppings:**

| | |
|---|---|
| 2 | plum tomatoes, finely chopped |
| 2 | green onions, thinly sliced |
| 1 tbsp / 15 mL | balsamic vinegar |
| 1 tbsp / 15 mL | olive oil |
| few drops | Tabasco sauce |
| ¼ tsp / 1 mL | ground cumin |
| | salt and pepper, to taste |
| 14 oz / 398 mL | can refried beans |
| ½ cup / 125 mL | ricotta cheese |
| ½ cup / 125 mL | grated Cheddar cheese |

*To make the tortillas*, preheat oven to 350°F (180°C).

In a medium bowl or food processor, combine tortilla ingredients and blend into a soft dough. If too dry, add a little water. Gather dough into a ball. Turn onto a floured work surface and knead until smooth, about 1 minute.

Divide dough into 3 portions. Roll out each portion into a thin disk. Using a 3" (8 cm) round cookie cutter, cut out 8 tortillas per portion and transfer to a parchment-lined baking sheet, ½" (1.3 cm) apart. Prick tortillas with a fork to prevent or reduce air pockets.

Bake 15 minutes, or until golden. Cool on a rack. Place in an airtight container for up to 1 week or freeze for up to 1 month.

## MINI TORTILLA CANAPÉS (CONTINUED)

*For the toppings*, combine tomatoes, onions, vinegar, oil, Tabasco sauce, cumin, salt and pepper in a bowl.

Leaving a small border, layer toppings on each tortilla as follows:

| | |
|---|---|
| 2 tsp / 10 mL | refried beans |
| 2 tsp / 10 mL | tomato mixture |
| 1 tsp / 5 mL | ricotta cheese |
| 1 tsp / 5 mL | grated Cheddar cheese |

Place tortillas on a parchment-lined baking sheet and bake at 350°F (180°C) for about 5 minutes, or until cheese has melted. Serve warm.

Makes about 24 canapés

## SPICY TOMATO AND RED PEPPER SPREAD

*Spoon generous heaps of this robustly flavored spread on thick slices of crusty Italian bread. An unpretentious but satisfying appetizer.*

| | |
|---|---|
| 2 tsp / 10 mL | vegetable oil |
| 2 | medium sweet onions, chopped |
| 2-3 | garlic cloves, minced |
| generous pinch | EACH, ground ginger, cumin and allspice |
| ½ tsp / 2 mL | finely chopped jalapeño OR serrano peppers |
| 1 | red bell pepper, finely chopped |
| 14 oz / 398 mL | can stewed tomatoes |
| 1 tbsp / 15 mL | granulated sugar |
| | salt, to taste |

In a medium saucepan, heat oil over high heat. Add onions and sauté 3 to 4 minutes, until translucent. Add garlic, ginger, cumin, allspice and peppers and sauté 1 minute. Add tomatoes, sugar and salt. Bring to a boil, then reduce heat to low and simmer, uncovered, 20 minutes, or until thick.

Makes about 1½ cups (375 mL)

*Variations*: A topping of baby shrimp, crabmeat or bay scallops would make this appetizer extra special.

# REFRIED BEAN TOSTADAS

*Enjoy this popular Mexican dish as a snack or light lunch.*

**Tomato and Green Pepper Salsa:**

| | |
|---|---|
| 2 | medium tomatoes, finely chopped |
| ½ | green pepper, finely chopped |
| 2 | green onions, thinly sliced |
| 1 tbsp / 15 mL | chopped fresh cilantro |
| 1 tsp / 5 mL | granulated sugar |
| | salt and pepper, to taste |
| 2 tbsp / 30 mL | red wine vinegar |
| 1 tbsp / 15 mL | olive oil |
| | |
| 14 oz / 398 mL | can refried beans |
| ¼ tsp / 1 mL | cumin |
| generous sprinkle | hot pepper sauce |
| 8, 5 or 6" /<br>   12 or 15 cm | corn tortillas |
| | olive oil, for brushing |
| ½ cup / 125 mL | sour cream |
| 4 tsp / 20 mL | crisp crumbled bacon OR bacon bits |

*To make the salsa*, combine tomatoes, pepper, onions and cilantro in a medium bowl. Add sugar, salt, pepper, vinegar and oil. Toss.

In a medium saucepan, combine refried beans with cumin and hot sauce. Cover and simmer until heated through, stirring once or twice.

Brush tortillas with olive oil. Leave whole or cut into wedges. Toast in oven or toaster oven.

Layer toppings on tortillas as follows: refried beans, salsa, dollop of sour cream, bacon.

Makes 32 appetizer or 8 main-course servings

## APPETIZERS

# SWEET POTATO LATKES

*These nourishing little pancakes can be enjoyed all year round but they are especially popular during Hanukkah, the Jewish Festival of Lights. Serve them as an appetizer or side dish with the traditional applesauce or your favorite dipping sauce.*

| | |
|---|---|
| 4 cups / 1 L | shredded sweet potato |
| 4 | green onions, thinly sliced |
| 2 | eggs, beaten |
| 2 tbsp / 30 mL | sour cream OR plain yogurt |
| ¼ cup / 60 mL | unbleached flour |
| ¼ cup / 60 mL | dried bread crumbs |
| 1 tsp / 5 mL | ground cumin (optional) |
| | salt and pepper, to taste |
| | oil for frying |

In a large bowl, combine all ingredients, except oil.

Heat a large, well-greased frying pan over medium heat. For well- crisped latkes, use 2 tbsp (30 mL) oil per batch. Drop 2 tbsp (30 mL) of potato mixture per latke into the hot pan, shaping each with the back of a fork into a 3" (8 cm) circle, ½" (1.3 cm) thick. Fry 3 to 4 minutes per side, until well browned. Serve immediately or reheat in a regular oven or toaster oven to restore crispness.

Makes 12 to 14 latkes

# SPICY SAUSAGE RAVIOLI

*Pasta dishes are so versatile and most people love them. These tasty appetizers require few ingredients and can be assembled very quickly thanks to ready-made wonton wrappers.*

| | |
|---|---|
| 3 | spicy Italian sausages, casings removed |
| 1 | egg, beaten |
| 3 tbsp / 45 mL | chopped fresh cilantro OR parsley |
| 3 tbsp / 45 mL | chopped sun-dried tomatoes, in oil |
| 25-30 | wonton wrappers |

In a medium bowl, mix sausage meat with egg, cilantro and sun-dried tomatoes.

Lay wonton wrappers on a clean work surface. Place 1 heaping tsp (7 mL) of filling in center of each wonton. Brush edges with water. Fold over to make triangles and press edges to seal.

Bring a large pot of salted water to a boil. Gently drop ravioli into water in batches of 8 to 10. Return to a boil for 5 minutes. Remove with a slotted spoon. Repeat procedure with remaining ravioli.

Arrange 2 or 3 ravioli on each plate and serve as a first course with a dollop of sour cream and chives or Yogurt Cucumber Dip, page 146, or serve as a main dish with tomato sauce.

Makes 28 to 30 ravioli

# GRAVLAX WITH SWEET MUSTARD DILL SAUCE

*Whenever I have the opportunity to eat at a fine restaurant, I order dishes I don't usually make myself. Until recently, this was the case with gravlax, the Swedish delicacy which consists of raw salmon that has been cured with herbs and seasonings for a day or two before it is thinly sliced and served with a sweet mustard and dill sauce. Succulent! When a friend introduced me to a few simple gravlax recipes, I was tempted to try one. I'm so glad I did because it was simple and delectable. Here it is, the perfect appetizer for a large cocktail or dinner party.*

| | |
|---|---|
| 3/4 cup / 175 mL | salt |
| 1 cup / 250 mL | sugar |
| 2 tbsp / 30 mL | cracked white peppercorns |
| 2 tbsp / 30 mL | cognac (optional) |
| 6 | bunches fresh dill |
| 2-3 lbs / 1-1.5 kg | sushi-fresh salmon fillet, skin on |
| | Sweet Mustard Dill Sauce, page 86 |

*To make the gravlax*, combine salt, sugar and peppercorns in a small bowl.

Place 3 bunches of dill in the bottom of a rimmed dish just large enough to hold the salmon fillet. Generously rub skin side of salmon with seasonings. Place fillet skin side down on dill and rub remaining seasonings into fleshy side. Sprinkle with cognac, if using. Top with remaining dill. Cover loosely with plastic wrap and press salmon down with a couple of heavy cans. Let stand 2 hours at room temperature, then refrigerate 2 to 3 days, depending on thickness of fillet.

Shortly before serving, scrape dill and seasonings from fillet and pat dry with paper towels.

Place fillet on a cutting board and, using a long sharp knife, cut gravlax diagonally off the skin into very thin slices.

Serve with Sweet Mustard Dill Sauce.

Wrap any leftover gravlax in an airtight container and refrigerate up to 6 days or freeze up to 2 months.

Makes about 30 appetizer servings

# GARLICKY ESCARGOTS

*Tease your palate with this timeless French appetizer and be sure to have lots of fresh baguette to sop up the juices.*

| | |
|---|---|
| 4 oz / 115 g | can escargots |
| ¼ cup / 60 mL | butter |
| 2-3 | garlic cloves, minced |
| ¼ cup / 60 mL | finely chopped parsley |
| | salt and pepper to taste |
| ¼ cup / 60 mL | grated Gruyère OR Cheddar cheese |

Drain escargots and rinse under cold water. Pat dry with paper towel.

Melt butter in a medium frying pan over medium-high heat. Add garlic and parsley and sauté 2 to 3 minutes. Fold in escargots; season with salt and pepper. Heat through and sprinkle with cheese. Cover, remove from heat and let sit 2 to 3 minutes, until cheese has melted. Serve immediately.

Makes about 30 individual appetizers or 6 servings

# BAKED OYSTERS WITH GORGONZOLA CREAM

*Regarded as the most powerful of all aphrodisiacs, the oyster symbolizes virility, seduction and passion. Most often eaten raw with a squirt of lemon juice, oysters are also delicious baked, grilled, steamed or marinated. I recommend the following baked appetizer for the romantic dinner you've been planning …*

| | |
|---|---|
| 8-10 | shucked oysters, on the half shell |
| ¼ cup / 60 mL | crumbled Gorgonzola cheese |
| 2 tbsp / 30 mL | whipping cream |
| 1 tbsp / 15 mL | snipped chives, divided |
| | pepper, to taste |

Preheat oven to 350°F (180°C). Arrange oyster shell halves (use the deep halves) in a rimmed baking dish just large enough to hold them.

Using a fork, combine cheese, cream, 2 tsp (10 mL) chives and the pepper in a small bowl. Spoon mixture over oysters. Bake 10 to 12 minutes. Sprinkle with remaining chives.

Makes 2 servings

# WINE-SOAKED OYSTERS

*This chilled make-ahead appetizer is perfect for festive occasions. The marinade complements and enhances the flavor of the oysters. Warning – this can become addictive.*

| | |
|---|---|
| 5, 3 oz / 85 g | cans cooked oysters (not smoked), drained |
| 1 tsp / 5 mL | EACH, salt and lemon pepper |
| 2/3 tsp / 3 mL | mustard seed OR pickling spice |
| 1/2 tsp / 2 mL | crushed thyme leaves |
| 1/4 tsp / 1 mL | EACH, red pepper flakes and hot pepper sauce |
| 1/2 cup / 125 mL | olive oil |
| 1/4 cup / 60 mL | fresh lemon juice |
| 2 tsp / 10 mL | Worcestershire sauce |
| 2 tbsp / 30 mL | chopped fresh parsley |
| 1/4 cup / 60 mL | chopped green onion |
| 1/4 cup / 60 mL | dry white wine |

Place oysters in a medium bowl. Combine remaining ingredients and pour over oysters. Cover. Refrigerate overnight or up to 3 days to allow flavors to soak into oysters. Stir gently several times to combine flavors.

Serve oysters with melba toast or squares of thinly sliced pumpernickel bread.

Makes about 3 cups / 750 mL

# BLACK TIGER SHRIMP WITH COCKTAIL SAUCE

*The reason this old cocktail party standby continues to be popular is that it's absolutely delicious! Chilled shrimp dipped into a well-seasoned sauce are a simple pleasure for the senses.*

**Seafood Cocktail Sauce:**

| | |
|---|---|
| 1/2 cup / 125 mL | ketchup |
| 2 tsp / 10 mL | horseradish |
| pinch | EACH, ground allspice and coriander |
| squeeze | fresh lemon juice |
| 20 | large black tiger shrimp, peeled, cooked and chilled |

Combine sauce ingredients. Cover and refrigerate until ready to serve.

Arrange shrimp attractively on a platter. Serve with sauce for dipping.

Makes 4 to 5 appetizer servings

*Variation: For a* **Wasabi Shrimp** *appetizer, mash wasabi powder with light cream cheese and just enough mayonnaise to make a spread. Start with a small amount of wasabi and add to your taste. To serve, place shrimp, wasabi cheese and crisp rice crackers in separate bowls and let guests help themselves.*

# MARINATED GARLIC GINGER SHRIMP KEBABS

*You'll love these flavorful shrimp either as an appetizer or main dish. They look great and taste fantastic.*

| | |
|---|---|
| 8, 12" / 30 cm | wooden skewers |
| 1/4 cup / 60 mL | olive oil |
| 4 | garlic cloves, minced |
| 1 tsp / 5 mL | ground paprika |
| generous pinch | cayenne pepper |
| | juice of 1 lime |
| 2 tsp / 10 mL | grated fresh ginger |
| | salt, to taste |
| 32 | large shrimp (about 1 1/2 lbs/750 g), peeled |

Soak skewers in water for 15 minutes.

Meanwhile, combine olive oil, garlic, paprika, pepper, lime juice and ginger.

Thread 4 shrimp onto each skewer, piercing each one twice. Place skewers in a rimmed dish and spoon marinade over them, coating both sides. Cover and refrigerate 3 hours to overnight.

Just before grilling, sprinkle shrimp with salt.

Place skewers on a hot grill for 1 to 2 minutes per side, or until just cooked through. Serve warm or at room temperature.

Makes 8 appetizer or 4 main servings

*Pictured on page 87.*

# MINI TUNA OR CRAB CAKES WITH NIPPY TARTAR SAUCE

*Tasty nibbles, whether you serve these little cakes as an appetizer or main dish.*

| | |
|---|---|
| 3 | medium potatoes |
| 1/2 | medium onion, thickly sliced |
| 3 | garlic cloves, coarsely chopped |
| handful | fresh cilantro, chopped |
| 1 scant tbsp / 15 mL | minced chipotle chiles |
| 1/4 cup / 60 mL | bread crumbs |
| | juice of 1/2 lemon |
| 2 | eggs |
| 2 tbsp / 30 mL | yogurt |
| 2 tbsp / 30 mL | mayonnaise |
| 2, 71/2 oz / 213 g | cans tuna OR crab, drained and flaked |
| | oil for frying |

**Nippy Tartar Sauce:**

| | |
|---|---|
| 1/4 cup / 60 mL | yogurt |
| 2 tbsp / 30 mL | mayonnaise |
| 2 tsp / 10 mL | sweet relish |
| 1 tsp / 5 mL | horseradish |
| several shakes | hot pepper sauce |
| | salt, to taste |

Bring a small pot of salted water to a boil. Meanwhile, peel and cut potatoes into quarters. Add to water. Return to the boil. Cover, reduce heat to low and simmer about 15 minutes, or until potatoes are tender. Drain. Transfer potatoes to a large bowl and mash.

Place onion, garlic, cilantro and chiles in a blender and chop until fine but not puréed. Add to potatoes. Stir in remaining ingredients, except for oil, until evenly combined. Using heaping tablespoonfuls (22 mL), shape into 11/2" (4 cm) patties, 1/4" (6 mm) thick.

In a large frying pan, heat 1 tbsp (15 mL) oil over medium heat. Fry fish cakes, in batches, 4 to 5 minutes per side, or until browned. Serve immediately with sauce or place cakes on a parchment-lined baking sheet. Let cool to room temperature, then cover and refrigerate up to 2 days. Shortly before serving, reheat in 400°F (200°C) oven 4 to 5 minutes.

*To make the sauce*, combine all ingredients, cover and refrigerate up to 2 days. To serve, place a dollop of sauce on each fish cake.

Makes 25 to 30 mini cakes

*Tuna and Crab Cakes pictured on page 51.*

# GINGER TEA

*My daughter Lara and I have been fans of ginger tea ever since James Barber introduced us to it a few years ago. Ginger aids digestion, so this tea is particularly soothing after a big meal. I like the peppery tingle when I make it strong.*

| | |
|---|---|
| 8 cups / 2 L | water |
| 1 cup / 250 mL | brown sugar |
| 1/2-1 cup / 125-250 mL | thinly sliced, unpeeled gingerroot |
| 1-2 | lemons, halved |

Place all ingredients in a large stainless steel saucepan. Cover and bring to a boil. Reduce heat to low and simmer 30 minutes. Using a fork, squeeze lemon juice from lemon halves. Pour tea through a strainer into a large teapot. Serve hot or cold. Leftover tea can be refrigerated up to 3 days.

Makes about 8 cups (2 L)

# LEMONADE

*Is anything more refreshing than old-fashioned lemonade? Add mint sprigs to treat your eyes and your palate.*

| | |
|---|---|
| 1 cup / 250 mL | fresh lemon juice |
| 3/4 cup / 175 mL | granulated sugar, or to taste |
| 8 cups / 2 L | water |

Combine all ingredients in a pitcher and stir to dissolve sugar. Refrigerate until ready to serve.

Makes about 9 cups (2.25 L)

# HONEYDEW LIMEADE

*Refreshingly cool and thirst-quenching on a hot summer day.*

| | |
|---|---|
| 1 | ripe honeydew melon, peeled, coarsely chopped |
| 1/2 cup / 125 mL | fresh lime juice |
| 2 cups / 500 mL | water |
| 1/2 cup / 125 mL | granulated sugar |
| 6-8 | ice cubes |

Blend all ingredients in a blender until smooth.

Makes about 5 cups (1.25 L)

# TROPICAL SMOOTHIE

*A lazy, hazy summertime drink.*

| | |
|---|---|
| 1 cup / 250 mL | chopped pineapple |
| 2-3 | kiwis, peeled and quartered |
| | juice of 1 lemon |
| 3/4 cup / 175 mL | plain yogurt |
| 2-3 tbsp / 30-45 mL | liquid honey |
| 2-4 | ice cubes |
| 1-2 tbsp / 15-30 mL | tequila (optional) |
| 1 tbsp / 15 mL | shredded, toasted coconut (optional) |

Blend all ingredients, except coconut, in a blender until smooth. Pour into 2 glasses. Sprinkle with toasted coconut, if desired.

Makes about 2 cups (500 mL)

# ICED MOCHA SHAKE

*Super-cool, super-rich indulgence. Pleasure at its peak.*

| | |
|---|---|
| 3 scoops | coffee ice cream |
| 1 scoop | vanilla ice cream |
| 2-3 tbsp / 30-45 mL | chocolate syrup |
| 1/2 cup / 125 mL | strong coffee, cooled |
| 1/2 cup / 125 mL | milk |
| 4 | ice cubes (optional) |

Blend all ingredients in a blender until smooth.

Makes 2 servings

# GRAND MARNIER SUMMER SANGRIA

*The perfect cool, elegant cocktail on a warm summer evening.*

| | |
|---|---|
| 2 cups / 500 mL | freshly squeezed orange juice |
| 1/3 cup / 75 mL | granulated sugar |
| 1/4 cup / 60 mL | Grand Marnier OR other orange brandy |
| 3 cups / 750 mL | red wine |
| 2 cups / 500 mL | sparkling water |

In a large pitcher, combine orange juice, sugar, Grand Marnier and wine. Refrigerate until ready to serve, up to 2 days.

Just before serving, add sparkling water. Serve with ice cubes.

Makes about 8 cups (2 L)

*Variation: For a* **Sangria Blanco**, *substitute white wine for the red. Add orange, lemon, lime and/or peach slices, if you wish, to either sangria.*

# FESTIVE CHAMPAGNE COCKTAIL

*What better occasion to clink glasses with friends and family than during the Holiday Season? Cheers!*

| | |
|---|---|
| 1 cup / 250 mL | orange juice, chilled |
| 1 cup / 250 mL | cranberry juice, chilled |
| 26 oz / 750 mL | bottle champagne OR sparkling wine, chilled |

Combine orange and cranberry juices in a large pitcher. Just before serving, add the champagne. Serve in champagne flutes.

Makes 8 to 10 servings

# MULLED WINE

*Stave off the winter chills (and blues!) with a mug of this comforting hot wine .*

| | |
|---|---|
| 1 cup / 250 mL | water |
| 1/4 cup / 60 mL | sugar |
| 1 | cinnamon stick |
| 5 | cloves |
| 1/2 | unpeeled seedless orange, cut into thin wedges |
| 26 oz / 750 mL | bottle red wine |

Bring water to a boil in a large stainless steel saucepan. Add sugar, cinnamon, cloves and orange. Cover, reduce heat to low and simmer 15 minutes. Remove cinnamon, cloves and orange with a slotted spoon. Discard. Add wine to water in saucepan and heat through. Serve warm.

Makes about 4 cups (1 L)

# EGGNOG SUPREME

*Everyone tells me this is the best eggnog. Rich, creamy and decadent, it is pure pleasure.*

| | |
|---|---|
| 6 | egg yolks |
| 1 1/4 cups / 300 mL | sugar, divided |
| 1 cup / 250 mL | golden rum |
| 1 tsp / 5 mL | vanilla extract |
| 2 cups / 500 mL | milk |
| 1 cup / 250 mL | whipping cream |
| 6 | egg whites |

In a large non-metallic bowl, using a hand blender, combine egg yolks, sugar, rum and vanilla; blend in milk. Refrigerate 30 minutes, whisking mixture 2 or 3 times to melt the sugar.

Meanwhile, in a medium bowl, whip cream until soft peaks form. In a separate bowl, beat egg whites until stiff.

Using a whisk, fold whipped cream and beaten egg whites into yolk mixture. Serve in wine glasses. If making ahead, whisk eggnog again just before serving. Cover any leftover eggnog and refrigerate up to 4 days.

Makes 10 to 12 servings

*Pictured on page 191.*

*Pleasures*

PURE & SIMPLE

# SALADS, DRESSINGS, SAUCES, SALSAS & BUTTERS

# SALADE DAUPHINOISE

*I lived for 10 years in the Dauphiné region of France where walnuts grow abundantly and are incorporated into many popular dishes, including salads, stuffings for meats as well as confections. A simple vinaigrette, coupled with a handful of tasty herbed croûtons, will turn this salad into a mouth-watering appetizer or side dish.*

| | |
|---|---|
| 1 | large Boston (butter) lettuce, washed and shredded |
| 4-6 | slices bacon, cooked crisp, crumbled |
| 1/3 cup / 75 mL | walnut halves |
| 1/3 cup / 75 mL | cubed Gruyère or Cheddar cheese |
| 1-2 | shallots, minced |
| 1/2 cup / 125 mL | Herbed Croûtons, page 85, OR store-bought |
| | salad dressing of your choice, such as Lemon Dijon Vinaigrette, page 82, to taste |

Place salad ingredients in a bowl. Toss with dressing just before serving.

Makes 4 to 6 servings

# TOMATO AND CUCUMBER SALAD

*Very refreshing on a hot summer day, and outstanding with barbecued meats.*

| | |
|---|---|
| 2 | large ripe tomatoes, halved and sliced |
| 1 | cucumber, peeled, sliced thinly with a mandolin |
| 1/2 | sweet onion, finely chopped |
| | Sour Cream and Chive Dressing, page 85, to taste |

Place salad ingredients in a bowl. Toss with dressing just before serving.

Makes 4 servings

# MESCLUN, PEACH AND FETA SALAD

*Luscious flavors, gorgeous colors — a perfect summer salad.*

| | |
|---|---|
| 2 cups / 500 mL | mesclun mix |
| 2 | ripe peaches, peeled (optional), pitted and sliced |
| 2 | green onions, sliced |
| 8-10 | almonds, toasted and chopped |
| 1 tbsp / 15 mL | crumbled feta OR goat cheese |
| | |
| | Fresh Ginger Dressing, page 83, to taste |

Toss salad ingredients with dressing in a medium bowl. Sprinkle with a little more feta, if desired. Serve immediately.

Makes 3 to 4 servings

*Variations:* For a **Tuscan Peach Salad**, add 4 slices of prosciutto, sliced into thin strips. Toss with Balsamic Vinaigrette, page 82. For a **Peach Dressing**, purée 1 ripe peach and whisk in ¼ tsp (1 mL) EACH salt and red pepper flakes, 2 to 3 tbsp (30 to 45 mL) cider vinegar and ⅓ cup (75 mL) vegetable oil.

  *Pictured on the front cover.*

# CUCUMBER AND MELON MEDLEY

*Visually stimulating, refreshingly cool flavors.*

| | |
|---|---|
| 1 | English cucumber, peeled and cut into ½" (1.25 cm) cubes |
| 1 cup / 250 mL | EACH, cubed seedless watermelon, cantaloupe and honeydew melon |
| 1 | shallot, minced |
| 1 tbsp / 15 mL | chopped fresh mint |
| ¼ cup / 60 mL | fresh lime juice |
| 1 tbsp / 15 mL | sesame oil |
| 2 tsp / 10 mL | granulated sugar |
| | pepper and salt, to taste |
| several | romaine lettuce leaves, for garnish |

In a large bowl, toss all ingredients except salt and lettuce. Cover and refrigerate until ready to serve, up to 2 hours. Just before serving, toss salad with salt. Adjust seasonings. Serve on a bed of lettuce.

Makes 4 to 6 servings

# ORANGE, AVOCADO AND MIXED GREEN SALAD

*My partner Chuck impressed me with this refreshing salad the very first time he cooked for me. The perfect blending of sweet, mellow and tart flavors teased my taste buds and tweaked my curiosity about his talents in the kitchen. He has since cooked many tasty dishes for me, including Apple Wood-Smoked Salmon, page 128, and Smoked Back Ribs, page 169.*

**Red Wine Dressing:**

| | |
|---|---|
| 1 tsp / 5 mL | granulated sugar |
| ½ tsp / 2 mL | salt |
| | pepper, to taste |
| ¼ cup / 60 mL | red wine vinegar |
| ⅓ cup / 75 mL | olive oil |
| pinch | EACH, dried cilantro and basil |
| | |
| 2 | large seedless oranges, peeled and cut into bite-sized pieces |
| 2 | large ripe avocados, peeled, pitted and cut into bite-sized pieces |
| 4 | green onions, sliced |
| 4 cups / 1 L | mixed greens, loosely packed |

*To make the dressing*, combine dressing ingredients in a screw-top jar. Shake well before using.

Just before serving, place salad ingredients in a large bowl; toss with dressing.

Makes 4 to 6 servings

## LUNCH

# ASPARAGUS SALAD

*Not so long ago, a sure sign that spring had arrived was the appearance of fresh asparagus at grocery stores and markets. Now that it's available all year round, I use it quite regularly, most often as a salad.*

| | |
|---|---|
| 16-20 | asparagus spears |
| 1 | small onion, finely chopped |

Balsamic Vinaigrette, page 82, to taste

Bring a large pot of water to a boil. Meanwhile, wash and trim asparagus of woody ends. Gently place asparagus in boiling water. Return to the boil and cook 4 to 5 minutes, until tender crisp. Drain asparagus and transfer to a serving platter. Top with onion. Spoon vinaigrette over warm asparagus. Let cool to room temperature. Cover and refrigerate until ready to serve, up to 1 day.

Makes 4 servings

# ORIENTAL CARROT AND LYCHEE SALAD

*Soft lychees (litchi) provide a sweet contrast to the crunchy carrots in this light rice vinegar dressing. Lychees are one of the most popular fruits in China.*

| | |
|---|---|
| 3 | medium carrots, sliced with a vegetable peeler |
| 20 oz / 570 mL | can pitted lychees, drained |
| 2 tbsp / 30 mL | raisins |
| 2 | green onions, thinly sliced |
| 1 tsp / 5 mL | grated fresh ginger |
| 2-3 tbsp / 30-45 mL | rice vinegar |
| 1 tbsp / 15 mL | water |
| | salt and pepper, to taste |
| 2 tsp / 10 mL | sesame oil |
| 2 tsp / 10 mL | toasted sesame seeds |

In a medium bowl, combine all ingredients, except sesame seeds. Cover and refrigerate until ready to serve, up to 24 hours. Just before serving, toss and adjust seasonings. Sprinkle sesame seeds over salad.

Makes 4 servings

# SPINACH, CARROT AND APPLE SALAD

*Crunchy apples, vegetables and nuts add texture and color, perfect with the light tangy vinaigrette.*

| | |
|---|---|
| 1 cup / 250 mL | matchstick-cut carrots |
| 2 cups / 500 mL | raw baby spinach, loosely packed |
| 1 | small apple, such as Russet, halved and thinly sliced |
| 2 | green onions, thinly sliced |
| ¼ cup / 60 mL | pecan halves |
| | Ginger Vinaigrette, page 83, to taste |

Place carrots, spinach, apple, onions and pecans in a salad bowl. Toss with dressing just before serving.

Makes 4 servings

# BOCCONCINI, SPINACH AND TOMATO SALAD

*Mild bocconcini is a classic complement to tomatoes.*

| | |
|---|---|
| 1 cup / 250 mL | raw baby spinach |
| 3-4 | bocconcini*, quartered |
| 4 | cherry tomatoes, halved |
| 1 | green onion, chopped |
| 1-2 tbsp / 15-30 mL | toasted pine nuts |
| | Balsamic Vinaigrette, page 82, to taste |

Arrange spinach leaves attractively on a small serving platter. Spread bocconcini and tomatoes over spinach. Sprinkle with onions and pine nuts. Spoon vinaigrette over salad. Serve immediately.

Makes 2 servings

* Bocconcini, usually about 1" (2.5 cm) in diameter, are small morsels of fresh mozzarella. Bocconcini also means "mouthful" in Italian, e.g., a mouth-watering dish of veal stew could be called *Bocconcini di Vitello*.

# GRAPE, BASIL AND NASTURTIUM SALAD

*If you have an abundance of basil and nasturtiums in your vegetable garden, you might like to try this combination of sweet and savory flavors. The peppery bite of nasturtium leaves and flowers is a gutsy complement to the sweetness of the grapes.*

| | |
|---|---|
| 1 cup / 250 mL | seedless green OR red grapes, cut in half |
| 2 tbsp / 30 mL | walnut pieces, toasted |
| 1 cup / 250 mL | shredded basil leaves |
| 1 cup / 250 mL | nasturtium leaves |
| | nasturtium flowers, for garnish |
| | Balsamic Vinaigrette, page 82, OR your favorite salad dressing, to taste |

Toss salad ingredients with dressing in a large bowl. Garnish with flowers. Serve immediately.

Makes 3 to 4 servings

# FENNEL, ORANGE AND PECAN SALAD

*Crunchy fennel and pecans with a burst of orange ... simple pleasures.*

| | |
|---|---|
| 1 | orange, peeled and cut into bite-sized pieces |
| ½ | fennel bulb, ends trimmed and thinly sliced crosswise |
| 1 | green onion, thinly sliced |
| ¼ cup / 60 mL | pecan halves |
| | Balsamic Vinaigrette, page 82, to taste |

Toss salad ingredients with vinaigrette in a medium bowl. Cover and refrigerate until ready to serve, up to 2 hours.

Makes 2 to 4 servings

*Pictured on page 121.*

# MANGO AND SWEET RED PEPPER SALAD

*Colorful, visually appetizing, sweet and sour flavors. Can be served as a salad or salsa.*

| | |
|---|---|
| 2 | ripe mangoes, peeled, pitted and julienned |
| 1 | red bell pepper, julienned |
| 2 | green onions, sliced |
| | |
| | Fresh Ginger Vinaigrette, page 83 |

Toss salad ingredients with dressing in a medium bowl. Cover and refrigerate until ready to serve, up to 1 day. Serve on a bed of mixed greens if you wish.

Makes 4 servings

*Pictured on page 87.*

# BROCCOLI, APPLE AND CRANBERRY SALAD

*To intensify flavors, let this crunchy salad marinate for a day before serving.*

| | |
|---|---|
| 2 cups / 500 mL | chopped broccoli |
| 1 | apple, peeled, cored and chopped |
| 2 tbsp / 30 mL | dried cranberries |
| 2 tbsp / 30 mL | chopped walnuts OR pecans |
| 2 tbsp / 30 mL | chopped onion |
| | |
| | Balsamic Vinaigrette, page 82, OR your favorite salad dressing, to taste |

Toss salad ingredients with dressing in a medium bowl. Cover and refrigerate until ready to serve, up to 2 days.

Makes 3 to 4 servings

*Pictured on page 69.*

# LENTIL, ARTICHOKE AND TOMATO SALAD

*Make this delicious salad a day ahead so flavors can blend. Perfect for brunch.*

| | |
|---|---|
| 2, 19 oz / 540 mL | cans lentils, drained |
| 6 oz / 170 mL | jar marinated artichoke hearts, drained and quartered |
| 3-4 | green onions, thinly sliced |
| 8-10 | grape tomatoes, halved OR 6 cherry tomatoes, quartered |
| | Balsamic OR Lemon Dijon Vinaigrette, page 82 |

Place all salad ingredients in a large bowl. Toss with vinaigrette. Cover and refrigerate up to 1 day. Adjust seasonings just before serving.

Makes 8 to 10 servings

*Variations: Substitute red or white kidney or navy beans for the lentils.*

# BARLEY AND BLACK BEAN SALAD

*Jump-start this nutritious salad by dressing it a day or two ahead to let the flavors blend and free up your time. A hearty flavorful brunch, lunch or picnic dish.*

| | |
|---|---|
| 1 cup / 250 mL | pearl barley |
| 19 oz / 540 mL | can black beans, rinsed and drained |
| 1 | red bell pepper, finely chopped |
| 2-3 | green onions, thinly sliced |
| generous pinch | EACH, cumin, salt and pepper |
| | Balsamic Vinaigrette, page 82 |

Cook barley in a large pot of boiling water for about 1½ hours, or until tender. Drain.

Transfer barley to a large bowl. Add remaining salad ingredients and toss with vinaigrette. Cover and refrigerate up to 3 days. Adjust seasonings just before serving.

Makes about 10 servings

# RED BEET SALAD

*Make this delicious salad a day ahead to give it time for the flavors to blend. Beets require a long time to cook, so it's a good idea to cook more than you need, especially since beet salad keeps at least one week in the fridge.*

| | |
|---|---|
| 2 lbs / 1 kg | red beets, washed |
| 2 tsp / 10 mL | granulated sugar |
| ½ | medium sweet onion, finely chopped |
| | Balsamic Vinaigrette, page 82, to taste |

Bring a large saucepan half-filled with water to a boil. Add beets and return to a boil. Cover, reduce heat to low and simmer about 1 hour, or until beets are tender.* Drain. Trim and peel beets as soon as they are cool enough to handle.

Thinly slice beets and transfer them to a salad bowl. Add sugar, onions and dressing and toss to coat. Let cool to room temperature, cover and refrigerate. Adjust seasonings before serving.

Makes about 4 cups (1 L)

* Insert a toothpick to determine tenderness.

*The rich color of beets indicates their powerful cancer-fighting properties. Especially effective against colon and stomach cancers, beets also help protect against heart disease and birth defects. They provide antioxidant protection and also help to lower LDL (bad) cholesterol while increasing the HDL (good) cholesterol. For expectant mothers, 1 cup (250 mL) of cooked beets provides a third of the daily requirement of folate, which is necessary for the proper development of infants. As well as an excellent source of folate, beets are a very good source of manganese and potassium.*

*Choose small, firm, smooth-skinned beets. Refrigerate beets, unwashed, for up to 1 month. Leave about 2" (5 cm) of stem and store greens separately. Cook greens within 3 to 4 days. Add grated raw beets to salads and use as a garnish for soups.*

# TOFU SLAW

*This lovely protein-rich salad gets its delicate flavors from the Asian vinaigrette dressing. There's no need to marinate the tofu. Grating it allows it to absorb the flavors of the other ingredients as soon as it's mixed with them.*

| | |
|---|---|
| 1 cup / 250 mL | grated extra-firm tofu* |
| 2 | green onions, thinly sliced |
| ½ tsp / 2 mL | granulated sugar |
| 2 tsp / 10 mL | rice vinegar |
| 2 tsp / 10 mL | sesame oil |
| ½ tsp / 2 mL | soy sauce |
| | pepper, to taste |
| several | Romaine lettuce leaves, for garnish |
| 2 tsp / 10 mL | toasted sesame seeds |
| 2 tbsp / 30 mL | dried bonito flakes** (optional) |

Toss tofu, onions, sugar, vinegar, oil, soy sauce and pepper together in a small bowl. Transfer to a platter lined with Romaine lettuce. Just before serving, sprinkle with sesame seeds and bonito flakes, if using.

Makes 4 small servings

* To grate, use the largest holes on the grater.

** Bonito are small, intensely flavored tuna. Often used in Japanese recipes, dried flaked bonito can be found in Asian grocery stores.

# OLD-FASHIONED COLESLAW

*Crisp shredded cabbage tossed in a sweet and sour dressing. Refreshingly tangy; traditionally simple.*

**Oil and Vinegar Dressing:**

| | |
|---|---|
| ⅓ cup / 75 mL | white vinegar |
| ⅓ cup / 75 mL | granulated sugar |
| ⅓ cup / 75 mL | vegetable oil |
| | salt and pepper, to taste |
| | |
| 1 lb / 500 g | shredded cabbage |

*To make the dressing*, combine dressing ingredients in a screw-top jar. Shake well.

Toss cabbage with dressing in a medium bowl. Cover and refrigerate until ready to serve, up to 2 days.

Makes 6 to 8 servings

# EGG AND WATERCRESS SALAD

*Most people think of watercress as a garnish for meats and soups. I enjoy its tender leaves mixed with sliced hard-boiled eggs and tossed in Balsamic Vinaigrette.*

| | |
|---|---|
| 1 | bunch watercress (enough for 4 servings), ends trimmed |
| 2 | hard-boiled eggs, peeled and sliced |
| | Balsamic Vinaigrette, page 82, to taste |

Place watercress and eggs in a salad bowl. Toss with dressing just before serving.

Makes 4 servings

# ASIAN NOODLE SALAD WITH LIME AND GINGER DRESSING

*An all-natural, nourishing yet easy-on-the-waistline kind of meal, all in one bowl.*

**Lime and Ginger Dressing:**

| | |
|---|---|
| 1 tbsp / 15 mL | grated fresh ginger |
| 2 | garlic cloves, minced |
| 1 tbsp / 15 mL | brown sugar |
| ¼ cup / 60 mL | seasoned rice vinegar |
| 3 tbsp / 45 mL | soy sauce |
| | grated zest of 1 lime |
| 2 tbsp / 30 mL | fresh lime juice |
| 2 tbsp / 30 mL | sesame oil |
| | hot pepper sauce, to taste |
| | |
| 1 lb / 500 g | Chinese rice noodles |
| 2 tbsp / 30 mL | vegetable oil |
| 1 | medium onion, thinly sliced |
| 2 | medium carrots, halved cross-wise and julienned |
| 1 | celery stalk, chopped |
| 1 cup / 250 mL | shelled edamame*, fresh or frozen |
| 8 oz / 250 g | snow peas, ends trimmed |
| 8 oz / 250 g | baby bokchoy, quartered |
| 8 oz / 250 g | shiitake mushrooms, sliced |
| 3 | garlic cloves, chopped |
| 2 tsp / 10 mL | grated fresh ginger |
| | salt and pepper, to taste |

*To make the dressing*, combine dressing ingredients in a small bowl.

Cook noodles as package directions. Drain, rinse and place in a large bowl.

In a large wok or frying pan, heat oil over high heat. Add onion and stir-fry 2 minutes, or until translucent. Add remaining ingredients and stir-fry 3 to 5 minutes, or until vegetables are tender-crisp.

Fold vegetables into noodles. Toss with dressing. Cover and let flavors blend 1 to 2 hours. Adjust seasonings just before serving.

Makes 6 to 8 servings

* Edamame (green soybeans) are available fresh or frozen. Raw, they are sold in the pod; steam for 20 minutes, chill and shell for salads or snacks.

# SALADE NIÇOISE

*This summertime favorite is a well-balanced meal in itself. Just add a freshly baked baguette and a glass of wine.*

**Balsamic Dijon Vinaigrette:**

| | |
|---|---|
| 1 tbsp / 15 mL | Dijon mustard |
| ¼ cup / 60 mL | balsamic vinegar |
| | salt and pepper, to taste |
| 1 cup / 250 mL | olive oil |
| | |
| ½ lb / 250 g | new mini potatoes |
| ½ lb / 250 g | green beans, trimmed |
| 4 cups / 1 L | loosely packed lettuce |
| ½ | medium sweet onion, thinly sliced |
| 8-10 | cherry tomatoes, halved |
| 16-20 | kalamata olives |
| 2, 7 oz / 213 g | cans solid white tuna, broken into large chunks |
| 4 | hard-boiled eggs, quartered |
| 3 oz / 85 g | jar anchovy filets (optional) |

*To make the vinaigrette*, whisk mustard, vinegar, salt and pepper together in a medium bowl. Gradually add the oil, drop by drop, whisking constantly until vinaigrette is thick. Adjust seasonings. Use immediately or cover and refrigerate up to 1 day. If dressing separates, re-whisk just before using.

In a medium saucepan, cook potatoes in boiling water for 5 minutes. Add beans and cook another 5 minutes, or until potatoes and beans are tender-crisp. Drain.

Peel and halve potatoes, then place them in a small dish. Spoon about ¼ of dressing over potatoes, toss and let marinate until cooled.

Just before serving, toss all salad ingredients with remaining vinaigrette. If salad is smaller than above, use less vinaigrette. Adjust seasonings and serve immediately.

Makes 4 to 6 main servings

# RUTH'S POTATO SALAD

*Whenever we have a family brunch, my mother contributes this delicious German-style potato salad. For maximum absorption of flavors, fold the dressing into the thinly sliced cooked potatoes while they are still warm.*

| | |
|---|---|
| 3 lbs / 1.5 kg | firm-fleshed potatoes, such as Yukon Gold, peeled and quartered |
| 1 | medium onion, finely chopped |
| ⅓ cup / 75 mL | EACH, white wine vinegar and olive oil |
| ½ cup / 125 mL | warm water |
| 1-1½ tsp / 5-7 mL | salt |
| | pepper, to taste |

Steam or boil potatoes in 1 cup (250 mL) water until tender, 15 to 20 minutes. Drain. When cool enough to handle, but still warm, slice thinly and place in a large bowl. Add remaining ingredients and toss gently to coat. Cover and let cool to room temperature. Adjust seasonings just before serving. Refrigerate leftover salad up to 2 days.

Makes 8 to 10 servings

# RICE, CHICKEN AND ASPARAGUS SALAD

*You can use leftover rice and whatever meat and vegetables you have on hand to make this simple nourishing salad. Peas are a good substitute for the asparagus and cold beef and pork are just as tasty as chicken.*

| | |
|---|---|
| 2 cups / 500 mL | cooked rice, preferably brown |
| 1 cup / 250 mL | chopped cooked chicken |
| 1 cup / 250 mL | cooked asparagus, cut into 1" (2.5 cm) pieces |
| 2 | green onions, thinly sliced |
| 2 tbsp / 30 mL | EACH, cashews and feta cheese |
| | Lemon Dijon Vinaigrette, page 82, OR your favorite dressing, to taste |

Toss salad ingredients, except for feta cheese, with dressing in a large bowl. Cover and refrigerate until ready to serve, up to 1 day. Just before serving, add feta, toss and adjust seasonings.

Makes 4 to 6 servings

# SALAD DRESSINGS

*Salads need to be dressed up for our taste buds to respond to them. Some of us like sweet, mellow accents while others prefer them sharp and acidic. But most of us probably enjoy a combination of these distinctive tastes. The following easy-to-make salad dressings cover a wide spectrum of flavors.*

## LEMON DIJON VINAIGRETTE

| | |
|---|---|
| 2 tsp / 10 mL | Dijon mustard |
| 3-4 tbsp / 45-60 mL | fresh lemon juice |
| 1 tsp / 5 mL | granulated sugar (optional) |
| 1/3 cup / 75 mL | olive oil |
| | pepper, to taste |

Combine all ingredients in a screw-top jar. Shake well before using. Cover and refrigerate any leftover vinaigrette up to 4 days.

Makes about 1/2 cup (125 mL)

## BALSAMIC VINAIGRETTE

*This is, without a doubt, the favorite salad dressing in our house. I make it almost daily. It's an all-purpose vinaigrette which enhances the flavor of just about any kind of salad.*

| | |
|---|---|
| 1-2 tsp / 5-10 mL | granulated sugar |
| 1/4 tsp / 1 mL | salt |
| generous pinch | pepper |
| 3-4 tbsp / 45-60 mL | balsamic vinegar |
| 1/4 cup / 60 mL | olive oil |

Combine all ingredients in a screw-top jar. Shake well before using. Cover and refrigerate any leftover vinaigrette up to 4 days.

Makes about 1/2 cup (125 mL)

**Variations:** *for even more flavor, add 1 crushed garlic clove, 1 tsp (5 mL) grated fresh ginger and/or 1/2 tsp (2 mL) dried herbs, such as basil, parsley or cilantro.*

# SOUR CREAM AND CHIVE DRESSING

*Creamy texture, light taste.*

| | |
|---|---|
| ¼ cup / 60 mL | sour cream (or yogurt) |
| 3-4 tbsp / 45-60 mL | seasoned rice vinegar |
| | salt and pepper, to taste |
| 2 tbsp / 30 mL | olive oil |
| 1 tbsp / 15 mL | snipped chives |

Combine all ingredients in a screw-top jar. Shake well before using. Cover and refrigerate any leftover dressing up to 2 days.

Makes about ½ cup (125 mL)

# HERBED CROÛTONS

*Liven up your favorite salad with these crisp savory croûtons. Sometimes I munch on them like popcorn or chips as they are delicious on their own.*

| | |
|---|---|
| 2 cups / 500 mL | stale bread (I like multigrain), cut into bite-sized cubes |
| generous pinch | EACH, ground coriander, ground fennel, dried oregano and dried basil |
| | salt and pepper, to taste |
| 2 tbsp / 30 mL | olive oil |

In a medium bowl, toss bread cubes with remaining ingredients. Place in a single layer on a parchment-lined baking sheet.

Toast in toaster oven for about 2 minutes or bake in a 350°F (175°C) oven for 15 minutes, or until croûtons are golden. Let cool, then serve or wrap in foil and refrigerate up to 3 days. Just before serving, toast croûtons again to restore crispness.

Makes about 2 cups (500 mL)

# SWEET MUSTARD DILL SAUCE

*A great flavor booster for grilled or poached fish.*

| | |
|---|---|
| ¼ cup / 60 mL | Dijon mustard |
| 1 tbsp / 15 mL | granulated sugar |
| ¼ cup / 60 mL | apple cider vinegar |
| | pepper, to taste |
| ½ cup / 125 mL | olive oil |
| ¼ cup / 60 mL | chopped fresh dill |

In a blender or food processor, combine mustard, sugar, vinegar and pepper. With the machine running, slowly add the oil through the feed tube. When thickened, add the dill and blend just enough to combine. Cover and refrigerate until ready to serve. Keeps up to 3 days.

Makes about 1 cup (250 mL)

# HONEY DIJON DIP

| | |
|---|---|
| ½ cup / 125 mL | sour cream |
| 2 tbsp / 30 mL | Dijon mustard |
| 2 tsp / 10 mL | liquid honey |
| 2 tbsp / 30 mL | apple cider vinegar |
| few drops | hot pepper sauce (optional) |

Combine all ingredients in a small bowl. Serve as a dipping sauce for meats and vegetables.

Makes just under 1 cup (250 mL)

## SEAFOOD DINNER

*Maple Syrup-Laced Baked Sweet Potato Fries,* page 111

*Marinated Garlic Ginger Shrimp Kebabs,* page 59

*Mango and Sweet Red Pepper Salad,* page 74

# QUICK RED PEPPER SAUCE

*A tasty condiment for hamburgers and other meats.*

| | |
|---|---|
| ¼ cup / 60 mL | mayonnaise |
| ¼ cup / 60 mL | minced roasted red peppers |
| 1 | shallot, minced |
| 1 tsp / 5 mL | balsamic vinegar |
| pinch | EACH, dried oregano and ground coriander |

Combine all ingredients in a food processor and purée until smooth. Cover and refrigerate until ready to serve, up to 2 days.

Makes about ¾ cup (175 mL)

# WALNUT PESTO

*Dress up pasta, meat or fish with this nutty, mellow-tasting pesto.*

| | |
|---|---|
| ³/₄ cup / 175 mL | walnut pieces |
| ³/₄ cup / 175 mL | loosely packed fresh basil leaves |
| 4-6 | garlic cloves, coarsely chopped |
| ½ cup / 125 mL | grated Parmesan cheese |
| ¼ cup / 60 mL | walnut OR olive oil |
| | juice of 1 lemon |

Combine all ingredients in a food processor; blend until well combined but chunky. Serve immediately or cover and refrigerate up to 1 week.

Makes about 1½ cups (375 mL)

*Variations: To make* **Walnut Pesto Encrusted Shrimp Kebabs,** *thread large shrimp onto wooden skewers. Sprinkle them with a little lemon juice, then lather with Walnut Pesto. Refrigerate 2 to 6 hours. Cook on a hot grill for 1 to 2 minutes per side, or until just cooked through.*

*For* **Almond Pesto,** *substitute chopped almonds for the walnuts.*

# MANGO AND TOMATO SALSA

*Sweet ripe mango tossed in a tangy dressing is sure to add a spark to grilled meats and seafood.*

| | |
|---|---|
| 1 | ripe mango, peeled, pitted and chopped |
| 1 | medium tomato, chopped |
| 1/2 | medium sweet onion, chopped |
| 1 tsp / 5 mL | dried tarragon |
| 1 tsp / 5 mL | granulated sugar |
| | salt and pepper, to taste |
| 1-2 tbsp / 15-30 mL | balsamic vinegar |
| 1 tbsp / 15 mL | olive oil |

Toss all ingredients in a small bowl. Cover and refrigerate up to 2 days.

Makes about 1 cup (250 mL)

**Variations:** For **Peach and Tomato Salsa,** *substitute ripe juicy peaches or nectarines for mangoes.*

# RED ONION AND TOMATO SALSA

*Fresh ingredients make this simple salsa a flavorful accompaniment to both meat and vegetarian dishes.*

| | |
|---|---|
| 1 | medium red onion, chopped |
| 1 | large tomato, chopped |
| 1 tbsp / 15 mL | chopped fresh parsley |
| 1 tbsp / 15 mL | chopped fresh mint leaves |
| 2 tsp / 10 mL | granulated sugar |
| | salt, to taste |
| pinch | chili powder |
| 1-2 tbsp / 15-30 mL | balsamic vinegar |
| 2 tsp / 10 mL | olive oil |

Toss all ingredients in a medium bowl. Refrigerate until ready to serve, up to 1 day.

Makes about 1½ cups (375 mL)

# APPLE AND CRANBERRY SALSA

*Try this sweet and tart salsa instead of the usual cranberry sauce with your next turkey dinner. Goes well with pork, too.*

| | |
|---|---|
| 1 | medium sweet onion, chopped |
| 2 | apples, peeled, cored and chopped |
| ½ cup / 125 mL | dried cranberries |
| 1 tbsp / 15 mL | brown sugar |
| ¼ cup / 60 mL | fresh orange juice |
| 1 tbsp / 15 mL | fresh lemon juice |
| 1 tsp / 5 mL | chopped fresh mint |
| | salt and pepper, to taste |

Combine all ingredients in a medium bowl. Cover, refrigerate and let marinate 1 to 4 hours. Adjust seasonings just before serving.

Makes 2 to 3 cups (500 to 750 mL)


# ORANGE CRANBERRY SAUCE

*Give traditional cranberry sauce an extra burst of flavor by adding some orange juice and zest. Thanksgiving and Christmas are busy times, so try making this sauce ahead. It keeps well in the refrigerator for at least two weeks. Whenever I have leftover sauce, I freeze it in small batches to serve with roast chicken or pork at a later date.*

| | |
|---|---|
| 12 oz / 340 g | pkg fresh or frozen cranberries, rinsed |
| 1 cup / 250 mL | granulated sugar |
| 1 cup / 250 mL | orange juice |
| | grated zest of 1 orange |

In a medium saucepan, bring all ingredients to a boil. Reduce heat and simmer 5 minutes, stirring occasionally. Remove from heat and let cool to room temperature. Cover and refrigerate until ready to serve.

Makes about 2 cups (500 mL)

# APRICOT AND APPLE CHUTNEY

*A combination of sweet apricots, apples and condiments, simmered in apple cider vinegar adds punch to grilled meats, rice and pasta dishes. Lots of ingredients but simple preparation.*

| | |
|---|---|
| 1 cup / 250 mL | quartered apricots, fresh or dried |
| 1 | medium onion, chopped |
| 1 | large apple, peeled, cored and chopped |
| 1 | large tomato, chopped |
| ¼ cup / 60 mL | granulated sugar |
| ¼ cup / 60 mL | apple cider vinegar OR white vinegar |
| 1 tsp / 5 mL | dried tarragon |
| pinch | EACH, cinnamon and ginger |
| | hot pepper sauce, to taste (optional) |
| | salt, to taste |

Bring all ingredients to a boil in a medium saucepan. Cover, reduce heat to low and simmer 10 to 12 minutes. Remove from heat and let cool to room temperature. Cover and refrigerate up to 1 week.

Makes about 2 cups (500 mL)

*Visually appealing, golden orange apricots are rich in vitamin A, which helps protect eyesight, and in vitamin C. The beta carotene and lycopene in apricots makes them important in heart disease prevention also.*

*Apricots came from China originally and arrived in North America in the early 1700s. Fresh apricots are delicious sliced into green or fruit salads or in cereals or pancakes. Dried apricots add a sweet Middle Eastern flavor to chicken dishes. Fresh apricots taste best when tree ripened. They should be slightly soft to the touch.*

# SWEET 'N' SOUR PICKLED ONIONS

*These crunchy taste boosters liven up any meat, fish or vegetable dish. They make a delicious garnish for sandwiches, too.*

| | |
|---|---|
| 2-3 | large Vidalia onions, thinly sliced |
| 1 | jalapeño OR serrano pepper, thinly sliced |
| ¼ cup / 60 mL | seasoned rice vinegar |
| | juice of 2 limes |
| 2 tbsp / 30 mL | granulated sugar |
| 1 tsp / 5 mL | mustard seeds |
| 6 | juniper berries (optional) |
| | salt, to taste |

Place onions in a medium bowl. Pour in enough boiling water to cover onions. Let steep 10 minutes. Rinse under cold water and drain. Return to bowl. Mix in peppers and remaining ingredients. Cover and refrigerate 24 hours. Leftover onions will keep up to 1 week.

Makes 3 to 4 cups (750 mL to 1 L)

*Vidalia onions, which originated in Vidalia, Georgia, are renowned for their juicy sweetness. Their season is typically May to the end of June. Other similar varieties are the Maui onion, Walla Walla, Oso Sweet and Rio Sweet onions.*

*Serrano chile peppers are about 1½" (4 cm) long, with a pointed end and very hot, full-bodied flavor. They start out green and become red when ripe. They are available fresh, canned, pickled, etc.*

# FLAVORED BUTTERS

*Do you like the flavored butters that are sometimes served in restaurants, with oven-fresh rolls, while you're perusing the menu? I occasionally make some at home by simply adding savory chopped herbs and spices or honey and nuts to fresh butter. They keep in the fridge for several days and freeze well, too. A sure hit every time you serve them! Also try some of the savory butters with steamed vegetables, meat and fish dishes. The sweet butters are delectable with muffins and fruit loaves. Following are a few of my favorite combinations.*

**Chive Butter:**

| | |
|---|---|
| 2 tbsp / 30 mL | snipped chives |
| ½ cup / 125 mL | salted butter, softened |

Using a fork, work chives into butter until evenly distributed. Serve at room temperature.

Makes about ½ cup (125 mL)

*Variations:* For **Herbed Butter**, *substitute chopped fresh parsley, sage, dill, cilantro OR basil for the chives.*

Try **Sage Butter** *for cold chicken, turkey or pork sandwiches; parsley or dill butter with egg salad, tuna or salmon sandwiches.*

**Garlic Butter:**

| | |
|---|---|
| 2 | garlic cloves, minced |
| generous pinch | dried parsley |
| | pepper, to taste |
| ½ cup / 125 mL | salted butter, softened |

Using a fork, work garlic, parsley and pepper into butter until evenly distributed. Serve at room temperature.

Makes about ½ cup (125 mL)

# FLAVORED BUTTERS (CONTINUED)

## Sun-Dried Tomato Butter:

| | |
|---|---|
| 1 tbsp / 15 mL | finely chopped sun-dried tomatoes (or more) |
| generous pinch | dried cilantro |
| | pepper, to taste |
| ½ cup / 125 mL | salted butter, softened |

Using a fork, work sun-dried tomatoes, cilantro and pepper into butter until evenly distributed. Serve at room temperature.

Makes about ½ cup (125 mL)

## Garlicky Wine Butter:

*A delicious roast beef sandwich spread or topping for a grilled steak or burger. A great use for leftover wine.*

| | |
|---|---|
| 1 cup / 250 mL | dry red wine |
| 1-2 | garlic cloves, minced |
| 1 | small onion, minced |
| 1 cup / 250 mL | butter, softened |
| 1 tsp / 5 mL | minced fresh parsley |
| | black pepper, to taste |

Combine wine, garlic and onion in a small saucepan. Simmer until wine mixture is reduced to half its volume. Cool.

Using a fork, work wine mixture into butter, with parsley and pepper, until evenly distributed. Serve at room temperature.

Makes about 1½ cups (375 mL)

# FLAVORED BUTTERS (CONTINUED)

**Roquefort Butter:**

*A zesty spread for crackers and sandwiches or topping for grilled chops, steaks and burgers.*

| | |
|---|---|
| ½ cup / 125 mL | butter, softened |
| ¼ cup / 60 mL | crumbled Roquefort, Gorgonzola OR Danish blue cheese |
| ¼ cup / 60 mL | chopped fresh chives OR green onion |
| 1 tbsp / 15 mL | fresh lemon juice |
| ¼ tsp / 1 mL | Worcestershire sauce |
| 1 tsp / 5 mL | brandy (optional) |

Place all ingredients in a food processor. Process until smooth and fluffy. Serve at room temperature.

Makes about ¾ cup (175 mL)


**Lemon Herb Butter:**

*Adds fresh flavor to steamed asparagus, artichokes and other vegetables or fish.*

| | |
|---|---|
| ½ cup / 125 mL | salted butter |
| 6 tbsp / 90 mL | fresh lemon juice |
| 1-2 tsp / 5-10 mL | grated lemon zest, or to taste (optional) |
| 2 tbsp / 30 mL | chopped fresh parsley, dill OR oregano |

In a small saucepan, melt butter and stir in lemon juice and zest, if using, and parsley. Refrigerate until about 30 minutes before ready to use.

Makes just under 1 cup (250 mL)


**Honey and Walnut Butter:**

| | |
|---|---|
| 2 tbsp / 30 mL | whipped honey |
| 2 tbsp / 30 mL | coarsely chopped walnuts |
| ½ cup / 125 mL | unsalted butter, softened |

Using a fork, work honey and walnuts into butter until evenly distributed. Serve at room temperature.

Makes about ½ cup (125 mL)

# FLAVORED BUTTERS (CONTINUED)

### Sugar and Cinnamon Butter:

| | |
|---|---|
| 2 tbsp / 30 mL | granulated sugar |
| 1/4 tsp / 1 mL | ground cinnamon |
| 1/2 cup / 125 mL | unsalted butter, softened |

Using a fork, work sugar and cinnamon into butter until evenly distributed. Serve at room temperature.

Makes about 1/2 cup (125 mL)

### Whipped Maple Butter:

*Fabulous on waffles, whole-grain muffins and breads, especially toasted.*

| | |
|---|---|
| 1 cup / 250 mL | maple syrup |
| 1 tsp / 5 mL | maple extract |
| 1/2 cup / 125 mL | butter, softened |

Using a hand blender, blend maple syrup and extract with butter until smooth. Serve at room temperature.

Makes about 2 cups (500 mL)

### Orange Marmalade Butter:

*Marvellous on muffins, biscuits, fruit loaves and toast.*

| | |
|---|---|
| 1/3 cup / 75 mL | orange marmalade |
| 1 1/2 tbsp / 22 mL | grated orange zest |
| 1/2 cup / 125 mL | butter, softened |

Using a fork, work marmalade and zest into butter until evenly distributed. Serve at room temperature.

Makes just under 1 cup (250 mL)

*Pictured on page 17.*

# STEAK SEASONING MIX

| | |
|---|---|
| 4 tbsp / 60 mL | coarse salt |
| 4 tbsp / 60 mL | paprika (try smoked for a flavor variation) |
| 2½ tbsp / 37 mL | EACH, ground black pepper and crushed, dehydrated onion |
| 1½ tbsp / 22 mL | EACH, granulated garlic, dried thyme, crushed red pepper flakes and rosemary |
| 1 tsp / 5 mL | ground cumin |

Combine all ingredients. Store in an airtight container.

Makes ¾ cup (175 mL)

# HOMEMADE BROWN GRAVY

*This basic, all-purpose gravy is easy to make and can be dressed up with herbs, spices, mushrooms and other flavorings.*

| | |
|---|---|
| 2 tbsp / 30 mL | vegetable oil |
| 1 | small onion, chopped |
| 3 tbsp / 45 mL | flour |
| 1½ cups / 375 mL | chicken, beef OR vegetable broth |
| 1 | bay leaf |
| generous pinch | EACH, ground coriander and dried basil OR lovage |

In a small saucepan, heat oil and brown onion over medium-high heat. Add flour to make a roux by stirring constantly until flour is brown. Slowly pour in broth, stirring until thickened and smooth. Add bay leaf, coriander and basil. Cover, reduce heat to low and simmer 5 to 10 minutes.

Remove bay leaf. Stir in meat drippings, if available, or a little more broth if gravy is too thick. Using a hand blender, blend gravy until smooth.

Makes about 1 cup (250 mL)

*Variations:* For **Hunter Sauce**, *reduce the broth to 1¼ cups (300 mL) and add ¼ cup (60 mL) red wine.*

*For **Mushroom Gravy**, sauté ½ cup (125 mL) thinly sliced or chopped mushrooms in a little butter or oil, then stir into gravy.*

*Pleasures*

# VEGETABLES, GRAINS & OTHER SIDE DISHES

# FRIED YELLOW TOMATOES

*Ripe firm-fleshed yellow tomato slices enveloped in a crispy bread crumb coating are a pleasant change from the unripened green tomatoes which are traditionally used to make this dish.*

| | |
|---|---|
| 1½ cups / 375 mL | unbleached flour |
| 2 tsp / 10 mL | salt |
| ½ tsp / 1 mL | EACH, pepper and ground paprika |
| 2 | large eggs |
| 2½ cups / 625 mL | bread crumbs |
| ¼ cup / 60 mL | grated Parmesan cheese |
| ¼ cup / 60 mL | sesame seeds |
| 2 tsp / 10 mL | EACH, dried cilantro and basil |
| generous pinch | nutmeg |
| 4-5 | large yellow tomatoes, cut into thick slices |
| | oil for frying |

Place 3 medium bowls side by side on a work surface.

In the first bowl, combine flour, salt, pepper and paprika.

In the second bowl, whisk the eggs.

In the third bowl, combine bread crumbs, Parmesan cheese, sesame seeds, dried herbs and nutmeg.

Dredge tomato slices in flour mixture, coating both sides. Dip slices into beaten egg, then place them on bread crumb mixture, again coating both sides.

Heat a large frying pan over medium-high heat. Generously oil pan. Fry tomato slices in batches, browning them on both sides for a total of about 6 minutes. Add more oil to the pan as needed. Serve immediately.

Makes 4 to 6 servings

# STOVE-TOP YELLOW ZUCCHINI AND TOMATO

*Use tender baby zucchini in this tasty dish, if you can find some. If not, regular-sized yellow zucchini, even green, will do just fine. Pair this with rice and serve with meats or seafood — delicious.*

| | |
|---|---|
| 1-2 tbsp / 15-30 mL | olive oil |
| 1 | medium sweet onion, chopped |
| 20 | baby yellow zucchini or 3 medium, chopped |
| 2-3 | garlic cloves, minced |
| 1 | large tomato, chopped |
| ¼ cup / 60 mL | spicy ketchup OR regular ketchup plus hot pepper sauce |
| generous pinch | EACH, dried oregano, basil and fennel seed |
| | salt and pepper, to taste |

In a large frying pan, heat oil over high heat. Add onion and zucchini; stir-fry about 5 minutes, or until lightly browned. Add garlic, tomato, ketchup and seasonings. Reduce heat to medium and continue to stir-fry until zucchini are tender-crisp, 3 to 5 minutes.

Makes 6 servings

*Zucchini, along with pattypan, crookneck and straightneck squashes, is a variety of summer squash which is related to both cucumbers and melons. Originating in Central America, they have been consumed for over 10,000 years.*

*Cancer prevention, including prostate cancer, reducing the risk of heart attack and stroke, reducing high blood pressure and preventing the oxidation of cholesterol are just some of the health benefits provided by summer squash. They are an excellent source of manganese and vitamin C; a very good source of magnesium, potassium, copper, phosphorus, vitamin A and dietary fiber.*

*Choose zucchini that are heavy for their size, with shiny, tender rinds. Medium size to slightly smaller summer squash will be the most flavorful. Store, unwashed, in the refrigerator for up to 7 days.*

# BRAISED SPINACH WITH MUSHROOMS AND ONIONS

*A tasty and healthy accompaniment to meats, lentils and chickpeas (garbanzos).*

| | |
|---|---|
| 2 tbsp / 30 mL | olive oil |
| 1 | medium onion, chopped |
| 2 cups / 500 mL | sliced cremini or button mushrooms |
| 2 tsp / 10 mL | soy sauce |
| 1 tsp / 5 mL | grated fresh ginger OR generous pinch ground ginger |
| 1 tbsp / 15 mL | rice vinegar |
| 10 oz / 285 g | pkg fresh baby spinach |
| 2 tbsp / 30 mL | toasted sunflower seeds (optional) |

In a large wok or frying pan, heat oil over medium heat. Add onion and sauté 3 to 5 minutes, until translucent. Add mushrooms and sauté 3 to 5 minutes, until lightly browned. Stir in soy sauce, ginger and rice vinegar. Add spinach, cover and simmer 2 to 3 minutes, or until spinach has wilted. Fold spinach into onion mushroom mixture. Sprinkle with sunflower seeds, if using.

Makes 4 to 6 servings

*The cremino (plural, cremini) mushroom, a brown version of the button mushroom, is more firm and more flavorful. The mature (larger) form of this mushroom has become known as the portobello mushroom.*

*Button mushrooms, originally known as champignons de Paris, were first cultivated in France. Mushrooms are fairly rich in B vitamins and potassium. They are cholesterol, fat and sodium-free and also low in calories.*

# ROASTED PEPPERS, MUSHROOMS AND ONIONS

*My daughter Bettina requests this dish when she and her family come over for dinner. The rich caramelized flavors of roasted peppers are fabulous with grilled fish, meats, risottos, pasta — virtually everything.*

| | |
|---|---|
| 3 | red bell peppers |
| 1 | orange bell pepper |
| 1 | yellow bell pepper |
| 1 | large Spanish onion |
| 16 | medium cremini OR button mushrooms |
| 1-2 tbsp / 15-30 mL | sesame seeds |
| | Balsamic Vinaigrette, page 82 |

Preheat oven to 400°F (200°C).

Cut peppers and onion into large chunks. Leave mushrooms whole.

In a large bowl, toss vegetables and sesame seeds with desired amount of vinaigrette. Transfer to a large parchment-lined baking sheet.

Bake 20 to 25 minutes, turning vegetables halfway through for even browning. Serve warm or at room temperature.

Makes 6 to 8 servings

*Bell peppers come in many colors: green, red, yellow, orange, purple, brown and black.*

*Rich in vitamins C, A, K and B$_6$, bell peppers are also very good sources of dietary fiber, manganese, folate and molybdenum. They give protection against free radicals and reduce the risk of cardiovascular disease and cancers of the prostate, cervix, bladder, colon, lungs and pancreas. The higher vitamin C content of red peppers helps to prevent cataracts and macular degeneration as well as rheumatoid arthritis.*

*Originating in South America, bell peppers are cultivated around the world. Store peppers, unwashed, in the refrigerator for up to 1 week.*

# LEEKS BRAISED IN TOMATO SAUCE

*"Poor man's asparagus" is what leeks used to be called. They were cheap and delicious and, unlike most vegetables, were available almost year round. Leeks, which have a mild nutty flavor, can be eaten raw in a salad but taste sweeter when sautéed or braised.*

| | |
|---|---|
| 1 lb / 500 g | leeks (3-4 stalks) |
| 2 tbsp / 30 mL | vegetable oil |
| 2 tsp / 10 mL | unbleached flour |
| 2 tbsp / 30 mL | water |
| ½ | chicken OR vegetable bouillon cube |
| 1 | medium tomato, coarsely chopped |
| 2 tbsp / 30 mL | tomato paste |
| | salt, to taste |

Trim leeks of ends and dark green parts. Slice into ½" (1.3 cm) rounds. Rinse thoroughly.

In a wok or saucepan, heat oil over medium-high heat. Add leeks and stir-fry until wilted. Stir in flour, then remaining ingredients. Cover, reduce heat to low and simmer 10 minutes. If all liquids have been absorbed, add 1 to 2 tbsp (15 to 30 mL) water. Return to a boil and simmer 5 more minutes, or until leeks are soft. Adjust seasonings.

Makes 4 to 5 servings

*Related to onions, shallots, scallions and garlic, leeks have a sweeter, more delicate flavor. The mild onion/garlic flavor is magical in creamy soups, salads and vegetable side dishes. Store leeks in the refrigerator for up to 5 days, in a plastic bag. Halve them and wash thoroughly before using. Smaller leeks are the most tender.*

*Rich in manganese, they are also a good source of vitamins C and $B_6$, iron and folate. They help to reduce LDL (bad) cholesterol and raise HDL (good) cholesterol levels, and stabilize blood sugar levels. Eating leeks twice a week may help to reduce the risk of colon and prostate cancers.*

*Originating in Central Asia, leeks were prized by the Greeks and the Romans who introduced them to Europe, including Wales, where they became the national emblem.*

# SWEET 'N' TANGY RED CABBAGE WITH APPLES

*Cabbage is a versatile and very good-for-you vegetable that can be prepared in a myriad of ways. In North America, we tend to eat it raw, mixing it with our favorite salad dressing to make coleslaw. Asian cooks like to quickly stir-fry cabbage, thereby preserving its crunchy texture; German cooks prefer to braise cabbage in a little wine or cider vinegar which gives it a deep rich flavor. The following recipe is of the slow-cooking variety and is one of my favorites. It is easy to make, but needs to simmer gently for 2 hours. I find it especially tasty with a simple pork roast, such as Pork Roast with Mushroom Gravy, page 168.*

| | |
|---|---|
| 2 tbsp / 30 mL | vegetable oil |
| ½ | large red cabbage (about 1½ lbs/750 g), cored and thinly sliced or shredded |
| 1 | medium onion, chopped |
| 2 | apples, peeled, cored and shredded or finely chopped |
| 1½ cups / 375 mL | chicken OR vegetable broth, divided |
| ½-¾ cup / 125-175 mL | apple cider vinegar, divided |
| | salt and pepper, to taste |
| ¼ cup / 60 mL | brown sugar |

In a large saucepan, heat oil over medium heat. Add cabbage, onion, apples, 1 cup (250 mL) broth, ½ cup (125 mL) vinegar, salt and pepper. Bring to a boil, cover and reduce heat to low. Simmer for 1 hour. Gently stir in ¼ cup (60 mL) broth and remaining vinegar; cover and continue to simmer for 1 hour. Stir in sugar and remaining broth (more or less, as needed for a moist consistency). Return to a boil. Adjust seasonings.

Makes 10 to 12 servings

# BRAISED CABBAGE AND NOODLES

*You may have sampled this side dish at a Chinese buffet. It is flavorful and very healthy.*

| | |
|---|---|
| 2 tbsp / 30 mL | vegetable oil |
| ½ | cabbage, cored and thinly sliced or shredded |
| 2-3 | garlic cloves, minced |
| 1 cup / 250 mL | chicken OR vegetable broth, divided |
| 1 tbsp / 15 mL | soy sauce, or to taste |
| | pepper, to taste |
| 2 cups / 500 mL | cooked rice or egg noodles |

In a large saucepan, heat oil over medium heat. Add cabbage and garlic. Stir-fry until cabbage wilts and starts to brown. Add ½ cup (125 mL) broth and the soy sauce. Cover, reduce heat to low and simmer for 5 minutes. Stir in a little more broth, as needed, and continue to simmer for 5 minutes, or until most of the liquid has been absorbed. Fold noodles into cabbage. Add a little broth if desired. Adjust seasonings.

Makes about 10 servings

*Cabbage is a very good source of vitamin C, omega 3 fatty acids, folate, manganese and vitamin B$_6$. It can help reduce the risk of breast, lung, stomach and colon cancers. Red cabbage contains 6 to 8 times the vitamin C of white cabbage and studies indicate it may protect against the risk of Alzheimer's Disease.*

# KALE AND HAM STIR-FRY

*Kale's image is changing from a largely unnoticed "wallflower" to a most trendy vegetable. In part, this transformation reflects the anti-cancer properties it shares with other cruciferous vegetables such as cabbage, Brussels sprouts and cauliflower. Also, it is easy to grow, needs very little attention, can be harvested in winter and appears equally comfortable in plain and fancy dishes. The following simple recipe is one my 85-year-old mother continues to prepare for our family a couple of times during the winter months.*

| | |
|---|---|
| 1 cup / 250 mL | water |
| 2 lbs / 1 kg | kale, stems removed and leaves chopped |
| 2 tbsp / 30 mL | vegetable oil |
| ½ | medium onion, finely chopped |
| 8 oz / 250 g | smoked ham, chopped |
| 2 | garlic cloves, minced |
| generous pinch | dried tarragon |
| | salt and pepper, to taste |
| 1 tbsp / 15 mL | white wine vinegar |

In a large saucepan, bring water to a boil. Add kale. Cover, reduce heat to low and simmer about 8 minutes, or until kale is tender-crisp. Drain.

Heat oil in a large frying pan over medium-high heat. Add onion and stir-fry 3 or 4 minutes, until just starting to brown. Add ham, garlic, tarragon, salt, pepper and kale and continue to stir-fry 3 to 5 minutes. Stir in vinegar. Adjust seasonings.

Makes 4 to 6 servings

# BRAISED FENNEL WITH CHEDDAR TOPPING

*This is one of my daughter Lara's favorite vegetable dishes, and one she frequently requests when she's home from university. The subtle anise flavor of fennel goes well with most meats and seafood.*

| | |
|---|---|
| 1 | fennel bulb |
| 1 tbsp / 15 mL | butter |
| 1 tbsp / 15 mL | vegetable oil |
| generous pinch | dried tarragon |
| | salt and pepper, to taste |
| 1 tbsp / 15 mL | sesame seeds |
| ¼ cup / 60 mL | broth OR water |
| ½ cup / 125 mL | grated Cheddar cheese |

Trim ends of fennel. Cut the bulb crosswise into thin slices.

Heat butter and oil in wok over high heat. Add fennel and stir-fry 3 to 4 minutes, or until lightly browned. Stir in tarragon, salt, pepper and sesame seeds. Add broth. Return to the boil; reduce heat to low, cover and simmer 6 to 8 minutes until tender-crisp. Sprinkle with cheese. Cover and simmer 1 more minute, or until cheese has melted.

Makes 4 to 6 servings

*Fennel bulbs, stems and feathery leaves are all edible. They can be eaten raw, in salads, or sautéed, added to soups and stews, etc. Rich in vitamin A, fennel also contains calcium, phosphorus and potassium.*

# BALSAMIC BRUSSELS SPROUTS

*Balsamic vinegar tones down the natural sharp flavor of these mini cabbages. A simple, great-tasting side dish.*

| | |
|---|---|
| 4 | slices bacon, chopped, OR 2 tbsp/30 mL vegetable oil |
| 1 lb / 500 g | Brussels sprouts, trimmed and halved |
| ¼ cup / 60 mL | water |
| 2 tbsp / 30 mL | balsamic vinegar |
| | salt and pepper, to taste |
| 1-2 tbsp / 15-30 mL | toasted sesame seeds |

In a wok or saucepan, cook bacon over medium-high heat until starting to brown. Add Brussels sprouts and stir-fry about 3 minutes, or until nicely browned. Add water and cover. Reduce heat to low and simmer about 3 minutes. Uncover and let any remaining water boil off. Increase heat to medium and add vinegar, stirring to coat sprouts. Cook 2 to 3 minutes. Add salt and pepper. Sprinkle with sesame seeds.

Makes 4 to 5 servings

# ITALIAN GREEN BEANS IN SPICY TOMATO SAUCE

*Italian or Roma flat/broad green beans are my favorite kind of green bean. They have that fresh "just picked" taste and the tomato sauce and peanuts in this recipe give them even more flavor. The narrower string beans are also delicious in this recipe. Enjoy these beans with grilled meats and Crispy Baked Fries, page 116. A delicious well-balanced side dish.*

| | |
|---|---|
| 1 lb / 500 g | (about 3 cups) Italian green beans, cut into thirds |
| 1 tbsp / 15 mL | vegetable oil |
| 1 | medium onion, chopped |
| 2-3 | garlic cloves, minced |
| 1 | large tomato, chopped |
| 1/3 cup / 75 mL | tomato paste |
| 1 | chicken OR vegetable bouillon cube |
| generous pinch | cayenne pepper |
| handful | salted peanuts |

In a medium saucepan, over high heat, bring 1/2 cup (125 mL) water to a boil. Add beans; cover and simmer 3 to 5 minutes, or until tender-crisp. Drain and rinse under cold water to prevent further cooking.

In a wok or frying pan, heat oil over high heat. Add onion and stir-fry 3 minutes, or until lightly browned. Add remaining ingredients, except for beans and peanuts, and simmer 3 to 5 minutes. Fold in beans. Continue to cook until beans are heated through. Sprinkle with peanuts.

Makes 4 to 6 servings

# MAPLE SYRUP-LACED BAKED SWEET POTATO FRIES

*Buttery soft texture, sweet mellow flavor — very comforting and healthy, too!*

| | |
|---|---|
| 3 | large sweet potatoes, peeled and cut into 1/2"/1 cm strips |
| 1 tsp / 5 mL | dried tarragon |
| 1 tsp / 5 mL | dried basil |
| 2 tbsp / 30 mL | sesame seeds |
| 3-4 tbsp / 45-60 mL | olive oil |
| | salt, to taste |
| 2-3 tbsp / 30-45 mL | maple syrup |

Preheat oven to 400°F (200°C).

Place potatoes in a large bowl. Sprinkle with tarragon, basil and sesame seeds. Add olive oil. Toss to coat evenly.

Spread potatoes in a single layer on a parchment-lined baking sheet. Bake 20 minutes, or until soft, turning once for even browning.

Sprinkle with salt and drizzle with maple syrup.

Makes 6 servings

**Variation:** *Try making this dish using butternut or acorn squash. It's delicious, too.*

*Pictured on page 87.*

# BAKED SQUASH

*This is my favorite squash recipe and it's also the easiest. To shorten the cooking time, I first cook the squash in the microwave oven for about 5 minutes and finish baking it in a regular oven.*

| | |
|---|---|
| 1 | acorn squash, quartered |
| 4 tsp / 20 mL | brown sugar |
| | pepper, to taste |
| 1 tbsp / 15 mL | butter |

Preheat oven to 400°F (200°C).

Place squash cut side up in a microwavable baking dish just large enough to hold it. Sprinkle with sugar and pepper. Dot with butter. Cook in microwave oven on high for 5 minutes. Transfer squash to regular oven and bake 30 to 40 minutes, or until lightly browned and soft.

Makes 4 servings

*Variations: For* **Maple Squash**, *substitute 3 to 4 tbsp (45 to 60 mL) of maple syrup for the brown sugar. Add 1 tsp (5 mL) of cinnamon to either version. If you are pressed for time, the squash can be cooked completely in the microwave, 15 to 20 minutes total, turning pieces every 5 minutes.*

# AU GRATIN SQUASH

*The French term "au gratin" means baked and browned in the oven, usually sprinkled with a bit of cheese. The following creamy squash casserole is sophisticated enough to be served as part of an elegant dinner. It can be baked ahead and reheated.*

| | |
|---|---|
| 4 cups / 1 L | cubed acorn squash |
| | salt and pepper, to taste |
| 2 tbsp / 30 mL | maple syrup |
| 3 | eggs, beaten |
| ½ cup / 125 mL | half and half cream OR milk |
| ½ cup / 125 mL | milk |
| ⅔ cup / 150 mL | grated Gruyère OR Swiss cheese, divided |
| several shakes | nutmeg |

In a saucepan large enough to hold a steamer basket, bring 1 cup (250 mL) water to a boil. Put squash in steamer basket and place over boiling water. Sprinkle with salt and pepper.

Simmer 10 to 15 minutes, or until soft. Drain. Transfer squash to a bowl and mash. Mix in maple syrup, eggs, cream, milk, half the grated cheese, nutmeg, salt and pepper.

Pour squash mixture into a buttered 2-quart (2 L) casserole or soufflé dish. Sprinkle with remaining cheese and a little more nutmeg. Bake at 350°F (180°C) for 1 hour, or until lightly browned and set.

Makes 8 servings

# GRATIN DAUPHINOIS

*Potatoes, garlic and lots of rich cream ... that's all there is to this scalloped potato dish which comes to us from the Dauphiné region of France. Irresistible pleasure!*

|  |  |
|---|---|
|  | butter |
| 4-6 | garlic cloves, minced, divided |
| 3 lbs / 1.5 kg | baking potatoes |
|  | salt and pepper, to taste |
| 4 cups / 1 L | whipping OR half and half cream* |
|  | nutmeg, to taste |

Preheat oven to 350°F (180°C).

Generously butter a large baking dish and sprinkle bottom with half the garlic.

Peel potatoes and slice into thin rounds. Spread potatoes in baking dish. Sprinkle with remaining garlic, salt and pepper. Pour cream over potatoes. Sprinkle with nutmeg and a little more salt and pepper.

Bake 1 hour 15 minutes, or until bubbly and lightly browned.

Makes 8 servings

* half milk, half cream is fine, too.

■■■ *Fat-free, satisfying and nutritious, potatoes are rich in "good" carbs plus 12 essential vitamins and minerals. A medium potato has more potassium than a banana and provides 50% of the recommended daily amount of vitamin C.*

# RÖSTI POTATOES

*Some foods really do taste best when prepared purely and simply, without all the trimmings that are supposed to make them look and taste better. To cook these röstis, all you need is a good frying pan, a little oil and some shredded potatoes. Fry them like pancakes until they are crisp and well browned.*

| | |
|---|---|
| 3 | medium potatoes, such as Yukon Gold |
| 2-3 tbsp / 30-45 mL | vegetable oil |
| | salt, to taste |

Peel and shred potatoes using the large holes on the shredder. Rinse potatoes under cold water and wrap in a dish towel or paper towels, squeezing out excess moisture.

Heat frying pan over high heat. Add oil. Carefully spoon potatoes into hot oil and flatten them with a spatula to form a large pancake about 1" (2.5 cm) thick. Reduce heat to medium and fry pancake for about 5 minutes, or until well browned. Turn over and fry other side for 5 minutes, adding a little more oil to the pan. Sprinkle with salt and cut into wedges. Serve immediately, while hot and crisp.

Makes 2 to 3 servings

*Variations: If you like, mix thinly sliced onion (about ½ cup / 125 mL) with the potatoes before frying. For a slightly decadent lunch dish or light supper, serve röstis with a dollop of sour cream and strips of smoked salmon.*

# CRISPY BAKED FRIES

*These scrumptious low-fat oven-baked fries, tossed with egg white, a smidgen of olive oil and herbs, are as crisp and flavorful as the conventional fries you crave but feel guilty eating. Do try them.*

| | |
|---|---|
| 6-8 | medium potatoes, cut into strips or wedges |
| 1 tsp / 5 mL | dried thyme |
| several shakes | EACH, paprika and ground coriander |
| 1 tbsp / 15 mL | olive oil |
| 1 | egg white, beaten until foamy |
| | salt and pepper, to taste |

Preheat oven to 400°F (200°C).

Place potatoes in a large bowl. Sprinkle with thyme, paprika, coriander and oil. Fold in egg white and toss to coat evenly. Spread in a single layer on a parchment-lined baking sheet. Bake 20 minutes, or until golden and cooked through, turning once for even browning. Sprinkle with salt and pepper.

Makes 4 to 6 servings

*Variations:* For **Spicy Fries**, *sprinkle with cayenne pepper before baking.*

# SWEET AND SAVORY GARLIC SMASHED POTATOES

*"Smashed" is easier and faster to make than "mashed" and the flavors of the two types of potatoes blend nicely. A light yet satisfying side dish with meat or fish.*

| | |
|---|---|
| 2 cups / 500 mL | chicken broth |
| 6-8 | garlic cloves, sliced |
| 4 | medium potatoes, such as Yukon Gold, peeled and quartered |
| 2 | medium sweet potatoes, peeled and quartered |
| | salt and pepper, to taste |
| 1-2 tbsp / 15-30 mL | butter OR olive oil |

In a medium saucepan, over high heat, bring broth and garlic to a boil. Add potatoes. Return to a boil, cover and simmer about 20 minutes, or until soft. Drain potatoes and garlic, reserving the liquid.

Coarsely mash potatoes and garlic. Gradually blend in as much of the reserved liquid as is needed. If mixture is too stiff, add a little more liquid. Sprinkle with salt and pepper. Fold in butter.

Makes 4 to 5 servings

# SIMPLE BEAN POT

*Traditional comfort food flavor without all the fuss. Canned beans taste great when simmered in an authentically flavored sauce.*

| | |
|---|---|
| 6-8 | slices bacon, chopped |
| 1 | medium onion, chopped |
| 3, 14 oz / 398 mL | cans navy OR great northern beans, drained and rinsed |
| 14 oz / 398 mL | can tomato sauce |
| 1 cup / 250 mL | chicken OR vegetable broth |
| ½ cup / 125 mL | barbecue sauce OR ketchup |
| ¼ cup / 60 mL | maple syrup |
| 2 tbsp / 30 mL | dark molasses (not blackstrap) |
| 1 tbsp / 15 mL | mustard |
| generous sprinkle | EACH, dried coriander and paprika |
| | salt and pepper, to taste |

Fry bacon in a large frying pan over medium high heat. When starting to brown, add onion and stir-fry 3 to 5 minutes. Stir in all remaining ingredients, cover and simmer over low heat for about 1 hour.

Makes 6 servings

*Variation: Beans are inexpensive and they taste terrific. Try the above full-bodied sauce with a variety of other beans, e.g., canned mixed beans or a can each of chickpeas (garbanzo beans), red or white kidney beans and navy beans or black beans. Add lentils if you wish.*

*Beans are a nutritional powerhouse. The history of their use goes back more than 10,000 years and spans the globe, from the Egyptian pyramids to the ancient Greeks and Britons to the Americas. Low in fat, beans are a good source of protein, complex carbs, iron, fiber, potassium, folic acid and other B vitamins. Dry beans will keep almost indefinitely if stored in a dry place, in airtight containers, at temperatures below 70°F (21°C).*

*Unlike other dried beans and peas, lentils don't require presoaking. They are tender after 30 to 40 minutes of cooking, about 50 minutes for purées. Like beans and peas they are an excellent source of vegetable protein and iron.*

# BLACKENED CAJUN CORN

*Would you like to add a little spice to your corn on the cob? Make this simple recipe as hot as you like.*

|  | salt, to taste |
| --- | --- |
| 1-2 tsp / 5-10 mL | cayenne pepper, or to taste |
| 1 tsp / 5 mL | ground cumin |
| 1 tsp / 5 mL | paprika |
| 8 | ears of corn, husked and cleaned |
| ¼ cup / 60 mL | butter, melted |

In a small bowl, combine salt and spices. Brush corn with butter and sprinkle with spices.

Grill corn on a hot barbecue for about 8 minutes, turning to brown evenly.

Serve with grilled hamburgers, chicken or your favorite seafood.

Makes 4 to 6 servings

*Native to Mexico and Central America, corn has been cultivated for about 7,000 years. Recent cancer research indicates that fiber-rich corn contains many anti-cancer phytonutrients, especially helpful in lowering the risk of colon cancer. Corn also contributes to heart health, lowers the risk of developing lung cancer and helps to maintain memory and produce energy. It contains vitamins B, $B_6$ and C, plus folate, phosphorus and manganese.*

# CREAMY POLENTA

*A nice change from the usual potatoes or rice, and easy to make. To achieve a soft creamy texture, let the polenta simmer very slowly.*

| | |
|---|---|
| 1 cup / 250 mL | cornmeal |
| 3 cups / 750 mL | milk |
| 1 cup / 250 mL | chicken OR vegetable broth |
| 1 cup / 250 mL | shredded Cheddar OR Swiss cheese |
| 4 slices | Cheddar OR Swiss cheese, cut in half diagonally (optional) |

Lightly butter a 9" (23 cm) pie plate.

Combine cornmeal, milk and broth in a saucepan. Bring to a boil over medium heat, stirring constantly. Reduce heat to low and simmer 10 minutes, stirring often until thick. Fold in shredded cheese and stir until mixture is smooth and detaches itself from the sides and bottom of the pan, another 10 minutes. Pour polenta into pie plate. When cool enough to handle, press down with your hand to make a smooth surface. Let cool to room temperature, then cut into wedges. If desired, top each wedge with half a cheese slice. If making ahead, cover and refrigerate up to 2 days.

Shortly before serving, broil polenta 3 to 5 minutes, until lightly browned, or heat in a microwave oven, about 3 minutes on high. Alternatively, brush wedges with a little olive oil and grill on a medium-hot barbecue for about 5 minutes, turning once.

Makes 6 to 8 servings

**Variations:** *For a traditional Italian version of Polenta, substitute ½ cup (125 mL) Parmesan or Gorgonzola cheese for the Cheddar or Swiss cheese. Water may also be substituted for the milk. Chopped onion (½ cup / 125 mL) sautéed in butter may be added to the cornmeal and liquid as it cooks.*

*Pictured on page 155.*

# HONEYED COUSCOUS WITH APRICOTS AND PEANUTS

*Preparation and cooking time add up to less than 30 minutes. A tasty accompaniment to grilled or roasted chicken or pork.*

| | |
|---|---|
| 1 cup / 250 mL | water |
| 1 tbsp / 15 mL | honey |
| | juice and grated zest of 1 orange |
| ¼ tsp / 1 mL | salt |
| | pepper, to taste |
| ½ cup / 125 mL | dried apricots, cut into strips |
| ½ cup / 125 mL | couscous |
| 2 tsp / 10 mL | butter |
| ¼ cup / 60 mL | salted peanuts |

In a medium saucepan, over high heat, bring water to a boil. Add honey, orange juice and zest, salt, pepper and apricots. Reduce heat to low and simmer, uncovered, for 3 minutes. Remove from heat, stir in couscous and butter and cover for 5 minutes. Fluff up with a fork and sprinkle with peanuts.

Makes 3 to 4 servings

*Pictured opposite.*

## CHICKEN – MAIN COURSE

*Honeyed Couscous with Apricots and Peanuts,* page 120

*Tandoori Chicken Kebabs with Yogurt Cucumber
Dip (Raita),* page 146

*Fennel, Orange and Pecan Salad,* page 73

# QUINOA, MUSHROOMS AND ONIONS

*A welcome alternative to rice or couscous, quinoa is a packed-with-goodness whole grain, rich in protein as well as in iron, calcium, potassium and magnesium. Its nutty texture and flavor are reminiscent of brown rice and it can be incorporated into many dishes, both hot and cold. The following recipe goes well with all meats; I particularly enjoy it with pork.*

| | |
|---|---|
| 2 tbsp / 30 mL | butter OR olive oil |
| 1/2 | medium sweet onion, chopped |
| 4-6 | mushrooms, thinly sliced |
| 3/4 cup / 175 mL | quinoa kernels, rinsed and drained |
| 1 1/2 cups / 375 mL | chicken OR vegetable broth |
| generous pinch | dried cilantro |
| | salt and pepper, to taste |

In a medium saucepan, melt butter over medium heat. Add onion and mushrooms and sauté until starting to brown, 3 to 5 minutes. Stir in quinoa and sauté 2 to 3 minutes. Add broth, cilantro, salt and pepper. Bring to a boil; cover, reduce heat to low and simmer 10 to 15 minutes, or until quinoa is tender. Fluff with a fork before serving.

Makes 4 to 6 servings

# SPANISH RICE

*Give your rice a little Spanish pizzazz by cooking it in some well-seasoned gazpacho. It's easy and delicious.*

| | |
|---|---|
| 1 tbsp / 15 mL | butter |
| 1 | garlic clove, minced |
| ½ | medium onion, chopped |
| 1 cup / 250 mL | Arborio OR basmati rice |
| 1 cup / 250 mL | chicken OR vegetable broth |
| 1 cup / 250 mL | gazpacho, page 15, OR store bought |

In a medium saucepan, heat butter over medium heat. Add garlic and onion and stir-fry 2 to 3 minutes, until translucent. Stir in rice and continue to stir-fry 2 to 3 minutes. Slowly add the broth, then the gazpacho, stirring until mixture reaches a rolling boil. Cover, reduce heat to low and simmer 20 minutes, or until liquid has been absorbed and rice is fully cooked.

Makes 4 to 6 servings

# PASTA WITH WALNUTS

*Toasted walnuts dress up and add flavor to this simple pasta dish. For a more substantial meal, toss with strips of smoked salmon, chopped cooked chicken, seafood, vegetables and/or cubed firm tofu.*

| | |
|---|---|
| 16 oz / 500 g | pkg of your favorite pasta |
| ¼ cup / 60 mL | walnut OR olive oil |
| ½ cup / 125 mL | walnut halves, toasted |
| ½ cup / 125 mL | Parmesan cheese |
| | salt and pepper, to taste |
| ¼ cup / 60 mL | chopped fresh cilantro OR parsley |
| ¼ cup / 60 mL | shredded Cheddar OR mozzarella cheese |

Cook pasta according to package directions. Drain. Transfer to a large bowl. Fold in oil, walnuts, Parmesan, salt, pepper and cilantro. Sprinkle with cheese. Serve with a salad.

Makes 4 main or 8 side servings

# PANFRIED PEROGIES WITH BACON, BASIL AND GOAT CHEESE

*Easy to make, nutritious and economical. Very popular with students who are doing their own cooking on a shoestring budget. If the goat cheese is unavailable or beyond your budget, substitute a little yogurt or sour cream.*

| | |
|---|---|
| 10-12 | perogies |
| 2-4 | slices bacon, coarsely chopped |
| ½ | medium onion, finely chopped |
| ½ | red OR green bell pepper, finely chopped |
| 8-10 | fresh basil leaves, shredded OR several shakes dried basil |
| 2 tbsp / 30 mL | unripened goat cheese |

Cook perogies in boiling water according to package directions. Drain.

Meanwhile, fry bacon in a medium frying pan until crisp. Remove bacon and set aside. Add onion and peppers to bacon fat in pan and stir-fry 1 to 2 minutes. Fold in perogies and continue to fry 2 to 3 minutes, until heated through. Sprinkle with bacon and basil. Dot with goat cheese.

Makes 4 side or 2 main servings

# SAVORY HERBED BREAD PUDDING

*Easier to make than dumplings, but similar in taste and texture, this "make ahead" side dish can be reheated just before serving. A thick robustly flavored gravy would be the "icing" for this pudding.*

| | |
|---|---|
| 1 tbsp / 15 mL | butter OR vegetable oil |
| 1 | large onion, chopped |
| 3 cups / 750 mL | cubed, stale white bread |
| 4 | eggs |
| 2 cups / 500 mL | milk |
| ¼ cup / 60 mL | chopped fresh cilantro OR lovage |
| 1 tsp / 5 mL | EACH, dried basil, tarragon and ground fennel seeds |
| ½ tsp / 2 mL | salt, or to taste |
| | pepper, to taste |

In a medium frying pan, melt butter and fry onion until lightly browned.

Place half the bread cubes in a parchment-lined 2-quart (2.25 L) casserole. Spread half the onions over bread. Repeat with another layer of bread and onions.

Whisk together remaining ingredients and pour over bread, gently pressing down with a fork to soak bread completely. Cover and refrigerate 1 hour to overnight.

Preheat oven to 350°F (180°C). Bake pudding for 1 hour, or until puffed and browned. Serve warm.

Makes 4 to 6 servings

# Pleasures
## PURE & SIMPLE

# FISH &
# SEAFOOD

# APPLE WOOD-SMOKED SALMON

*This dish, which everyone loves, has become my partner Chuck's "pièce de résistance." In fact, the "regulars" have come to expect it when they are invited to our house for brunch. Chuck wrote up the following recipe.*

| 2 lb / 1 kg | salmon fillet |
| | Sweet Mustard Dill Sauce, page 86 |

This recipe requires a covered kettle-type barbecue, and 3 to 4 handfuls of apple twigs of finger-thickness, 1 to 2" (2.5 to 5 cm) in length. Hickory chips work equally well, but these should be immersed in water for at least an hour before use.

I've always used a charcoal barbecue, but gas works well provided you have a small smoke box to hold the wood chips and/or twigs.

Pile the charcoal briquettes on one side of the barbecue and light. When white ash covers about ½ of the surface of the briquettes, spray the cooking surface with oil (well clear of the fire), sprinkle the apple twigs over the charcoal briquettes and place the salmon fillet, skin side down, on the side of the grill furthest from the briquettes (with gas, light one element and place salmon over the other).

Place cover on the barbecue, get a good book and open a beer. Cook for 1 hour to 1 hour 15 minutes without turning the fillet over. While the salmon cooks, the apple twigs will need to be replaced twice as the smoke diminishes.

Salmon may be served warm directly from the barbecue or cooked up to a day ahead and served cold. In either case, serve with Sweet Mustard Dill Sauce. To adjust quantities, simply use the ratio of 1 lb (500 g) of salmon for 3 people, while keeping in mind that leftovers are delicious because the smoky flavor is even more pronounced a day or two after it is cooked.

Makes 6 servings

# GRILLED MARINATED SALMON STEAKS

*Moist and flavorful, these steaks are very popular in our house. And only 30 minutes marinating time.*

| 4 | salmon steaks (about 2 lbs/1 kg) |
|---|---|

**Lemon Soy Marinade:**

| $^2/_3$ cup / 160 mL | soy sauce |
|---|---|
| | juice of 1 lemon |
| 1 tsp / 5 mL | granulated sugar |

Place steaks in a single layer in a rimmed dish just large enough to hold them.

**To make the marinade**, combine soy sauce, lemon juice and sugar and pour about half over steaks. Turn steaks over to fully moisten them. Let marinate 30 minutes.

Cook steaks on a hot grill about 5 minutes per side, or until just beginning to flake, basting several times with remaining marinade. A dollop of Yogurt Cucumber Dip, page 146, or Nippy Tartar Sauce, page 60, is delicious with these salmon steaks.

Makes 4 servings

*Pictured on the front cover.*

# SALMON BRAISED IN PROVENÇAL SAUCE

*You can free up your time by preparing this full-bodied Provençal dish a day ahead and reheating it briefly just before serving. For variety, you may want to toss in a few shrimp and/or scallops. Delicious!*

| | |
|---|---|
| 2 tbsp / 30 mL | vegetable oil, divided |
| 1 lb / 500 g | skinless salmon fillet |
| | salt and pepper, to taste |

**Provençal Sauce:**

| | |
|---|---|
| 1 | medium onion, chopped |
| 2-4 | mushrooms, sliced |
| 2 | garlic cloves, minced |
| 3-4 | ripe Roma tomatoes, chopped |
| ¼ cup / 60 mL | tomato paste |
| ¼ cup / 60 mL | spicy ketchup OR regular ketchup plus hot sauce, to taste |
| 12 | kalamata olives |
| 1½ tsp / 7 mL | Provençal seasonings* |
| 2 tbsp / 30 mL | chopped fresh parsley |
| 1 | vegetable OR chicken bouillon cube |
| ½-¾ cup / 125-175 mL | champagne OR dry white wine |
| 2 cups / 500 mL | loosely packed fresh baby spinach leaves |
| 2 tbsp / 30 mL | sour cream (optional) |

In a large frying pan, in 1 tbsp (15 mL) oil, fry fillets 1 minute on each side over high heat. Sprinkle with salt and pepper. Transfer to a plate.

**To make the sauce**, add remaining oil to pan over high heat; sauté onion, mushrooms and garlic for 3 minutes, until lightly browned. Fold in tomatoes, tomato paste, ketchup, olives, seasonings, parsley, bouillon cube and champagne.

Place salmon fillets on top. Reduce heat to low, cover; simmer 3 minutes. Using a fork or spatula, break salmon into bite-sized pieces. Fold into sauce.

Spread spinach leaves over sauce, cover, and continue to simmer 2 to 3 minutes, or until spinach has wilted. Stir spinach into sauce. Fold in sour cream, if using. Heat through. Serve over rice or pasta. Simply divine!

Makes 4 servings

* Herbes de Provence can be purchased as a commercial blend. It usually contains: basil, marjoram, rosemary, thyme, savory, sage, fennel and lavender.

# SALMON QUESADILLAS

*Versatile quesadillas make a satisfying meal anytime. Try this dish for dinner, lunch, brunch or even as an appetizer, cut into strips. Great with guacamole.*

| | |
|---|---|
| 4 | salmon steaks |
| | salt and pepper, to taste |
| | juice of ½ lemon |
| ½ cup / 125 mL | mayonnaise (more or less, depending on size of steaks) |
| 2 tbsp / 30 mL | plain yogurt |
| 2 tsp / 10 mL | puréed chipotle peppers |
| 2 | green onions, thinly sliced |
| 2 tbsp / 30 mL | chopped fresh dill OR cilantro |
| 4, 10" / 26 cm | flour tortillas |
| 1 cup / 250 mL | mixed greens |
| 1½ cups / 375 mL | shredded mozzarella and Cheddar cheese, mixed olive oil, for brushing |

Sprinkle salmon with salt and pepper. Grill or pan-fry salmon over medium-high heat until just cooked through, 4 to 6 minutes per side, depending on thickness of steaks. Sprinkle with lemon juice. Let cool. Remove skin and bones and, in a medium bowl, break up salmon into large chunks. Fold in mayonnaise, peppers, onions and dill.

Spread salmon mixture over half of each tortilla, leaving a 1" (2.5 cm) border. Top with mixed greens and cheese. Fold unfilled tortilla halves over filling, pressing to seal. Brush both sides with olive oil.

Grill tortillas in a panini maker, frying pan or grill, 3 to 4 minutes, or until lightly browned. Cut into wedges and serve warm.

Makes 4 main or 16 appetizer servings

*Variations:* For **Seafood Quesadillas**, *try other fillings such as chopped shrimp, crabmeat, lobster or scallops.*

# SEARED TUNA ON A BED OF CARAMELIZED APPLE, ONION AND FENNEL PURÉE

*Rare tuna's unbelievably tender texture is reminiscent of a perfectly ripened avocado. In the following recipe, its exquisite flavor is complemented by both spicy and mellow ingredients. A sensual eating experience!*

**Caramelized Onion, Apple and Fennel Purée:**

| | |
|---|---|
| 1 tbsp / 15 mL | butter |
| 1 tbsp / 15 mL | olive oil |
| 1 | large sweet onion, coarsely chopped |
| ½ | fennel bulb, coarsely chopped |
| 2 | medium apples, peeled, cored and quartered |
| 2 tbsp / 30 mL | granulated sugar |
| ½ tsp / 2 mL | salt, or to taste |
| ¼ cup / 60 mL | vegetable OR chicken broth |

| | |
|---|---|
| 4, 6 oz / 170 g | tuna fillets (about ¾"/2 cm thick) |
| generous pinch | EACH, paprika, coriander and cayenne pepper salt, to taste |

*To make the purée*, heat butter and oil in a large frying pan over medium heat. Add onion and stir-fry 5 minutes, or until translucent. Add fennel and apples and continue to stir-fry about 5 minutes, or until mixture is just starting to brown. Sprinkle with sugar and salt. Add broth. Reduce heat to low and simmer, uncovered, for 20 minutes, stirring occasionally, adding a little more broth if needed. Remove from heat.

Using a hand blender, purée onion, apple and fennel mixture, leaving it slightly chunky, if desired. Adjust seasonings. Cover and keep warm.

Season tuna with paprika, coriander, cayenne pepper and salt.

Sear tuna on a hot grill or in a frying pan, 1 to 2 minutes per side, leaving the center a rare pink.

Divide purée among 4 plates. Top with tuna.

Makes 4 servings

# PAN-FRIED TROUT FILLETS WITH BRIE AND CAPER SAUCE

*Condiments and herbs enhance the natural good flavor of fish. Here, mild trout fillets match perfectly with the buttery Brie and Caper Sauce.*

| | |
|---|---|
| 2 tsp / 10 mL | vegetable oil |
| 2 | trout fillets (about 3/4 lb/375 g) |
| | salt and pepper, to taste |
| | juice of 1/2 lemon |

**Brie and Caper Sauce:**

| | |
|---|---|
| 1 tsp / 5 mL | butter OR olive oil |
| 2 | shallots, finely chopped |
| 1/2 cup / 125 mL | chicken OR vegetable broth |
| 1 tsp / 5 mL | cornstarch |
| 1/4 cup / 60 mL | rindless, diced Brie |
| 1/4 cup / 60 mL | capers, drained |
| 1 tbsp / 15 mL | chopped fresh dill |

Heat oil in a large frying pan over high heat. Add fillets; sprinkle with salt and pepper. Fry 1 minute per side. Sprinkle with lemon juice. Using a spatula, transfer fillets to a platter.

*To make the sauce*, reduce heat to medium. To the same pan, add butter and shallots and stir-fry 2 minutes. Stir in remaining ingredients and bring to a boil; continue to stir until smooth.

Return fillets to the pan and cook another 3 to 4 minutes, or until sauce has thickened and trout is just cooked through.

Makes 2 servings

# SPICY BROILED RAINBOW TROUT

*Low-fat, great taste. And very easy to make.*

**Spicy Lemon Garlic Marinade:**

| | |
|---|---|
| 4 | garlic cloves, minced |
| 2 tbsp / 30 mL | olive oil |
| 2 tbsp / 30 mL | soy sauce |
| ¼ cup / 60 mL | fresh lemon juice |
| 2 tsp / 10 mL | granulated sugar |
| generous pinch | EACH, cayenne pepper, ground cinnamon, ginger and allspice |
| | |
| 4 | trout fillets (about 8 oz/125 g each) |
| 1 | lemon, quartered |

*To make the marinade*, pour marinade ingredients into a screw-top jar. Shake to blend.

Place fillets in a single layer in a shallow baking dish. Spoon marinade over fillets. Let marinate 15 minutes, then turn fillets over and marinate another 15 minutes.

Remove fillets from marinade and place in a greased baking dish. Broil fillets in a preheated oven 3 minutes per side, or until just starting to flake. Serve immediately with a sprinkle of lemon juice.

Makes 4 servings

*Variations:* Instead of broiling, fish can be grilled or pan-fried.

# DILL AND LEMON MARINATED BAKED SOLE

*Super easy, super light, super healthy. Tastes good, too!*

**Garlic Dill Marinade:**

| | |
|---|---|
| ¼ cup / 60 mL | chopped dill |
| 2 | garlic cloves, minced |
| | juice of 1 lemon |
| 2 tbsp / 30 mL | olive oil |
| generous pinch | paprika |
| | salt and pepper, to taste |
| | |
| 1 lb / 500 g | package frozen sole fillets, thawed |
| 3 tbsp / 45 mL | seasoned bread crumbs |
| 1 tbsp / 15 mL | butter |

*To make the marinade*, pour marinade ingredients into a screw-top jar. Shake to blend.

Place 1 layer of sole in a greased 9 x 9" (23 x 23 cm) baking dish. Spoon half of marinade over it. Add a second layer of sole and spoon remaining marinade over it. Let marinate 30 minutes.

Preheat oven to 400°F (200°C). Sprinkle sole with bread crumbs. Dot with butter. Bake 10 to 12 minutes. To brown top, broil for a minute. Serve with Nippy Tartar Sauce, page 60.

Makes 3 to 4 servings

# MOULES MARINIÈRES

*Always popular with seafood lovers, these mussels cooked in white wine and tomato sauce can be served either as an appetizer or entrée.*

| | |
|---|---|
| 14 oz / 398 mL | can stewed tomatoes |
| ½ cup / 125 mL | dry white wine |
| 1 tbsp / 15 mL | soy sauce |
| | juice of ½ lime OR lemon |
| ½ | medium onion, finely chopped |
| 2 | garlic cloves, minced |
| generous pinch | EACH, dried coriander, oregano and hot chili flakes |
| 1 tbsp / 15 mL | chopped fresh parsley |
| | salt, to taste |
| | |
| 2 lbs / 1 kg | mussels, scrubbed under cold water |

Fill a large pot with all ingredients, except mussels. Bring to a boil. Simmer on low, covered, for 10 minutes. Add mussels. Return to a boil until shells open, about 4 minutes. Discard any unopened shells. Serve immediately with a loaf of fresh crusty bread to soak up the juices. Pleasure, pure and simple!

Makes 6 main or 3 appetizer servings

# SCALLOPS IN CREAMY WINE SAUCE

*Flavor is not compromised by the speedy preparation of this sensational dish. One of the most important considerations in cooking scallops and other seafood is timing. If you want tender, not tough, brief cooking is the answer. This recipe can be made with shrimp as well as other seafood.*

| | |
|---|---|
| 2 tbsp / 30 mL | butter OR vegetable oil, divided |
| 20-24 | large sea scallops |
| 2 tbsp / 30 mL | diced sweet red peppers |
| 2 | green onions, thinly sliced |
| 2 tbsp / 30 mL | chopped fresh dill |
| pinch | EACH, dried oregano and basil |
| | salt and pepper, to taste |
| 1 tbsp / 15 mL | Dijon mustard |
| ¼ cup / 60 mL | dry white wine |
| ¼ cup / 60 mL | whipping cream |

In a large frying pan, heat 1 tbsp (15 mL) butter over high heat. Add scallops and sauté about 2 minutes per side. Stir in remaining ingredients. Bring to a boil; cook 1 to 2 minutes longer. Adjust seasonings and serve immediately over rice or couscous.

Makes 4 to 5 servings

# SPICY SCALLOPS FOR TWO

*A mouth-watering dish for an intimate dinner with that "special someone" . . . .*

| | |
|---|---|
| 2 tbsp / 30 mL | vegetable oil, divided |
| 12-14 | large sea scallops |
| | salt and pepper, to taste |
| ½ | medium sweet onion, thinly sliced |
| 2-3 | garlic cloves, minced |
| 3-4 | mushrooms, sliced |
| ½ cup / 125 mL | tomato sauce |
| ¼ cup / 60 mL | spicy ketchup OR regular ketchup plus hot sauce, to taste |
| ¼ cup / 60 mL | dry white wine |
| 2 tbsp / 30 mL | fresh cilantro, chopped |
| ¼ cup / 60 mL | herb and garlic cream cheese |
| generous squeeze | lemon juice |
| 1 | green onion, thinly sliced (optional) |

In a frying pan, heat 1 tbsp (15 mL) oil over high heat. Add scallops, sprinkle with salt and pepper, and brown them on both sides for a total of 2 to 3 minutes. Transfer scallops to a plate.

Pour remaining 1 tbsp (15 mL) oil into hot pan. Add onion, garlic and mushrooms and sauté over high heat until lightly browned, about 3 minutes. Stir in tomato sauce, ketchup, wine, cilantro, cream cheese and lemon juice. Bring to a boil; fold in scallops and reduce heat to medium. Cook another 2 to 3 minutes, or until scallops are still soft and just cooked through. Sprinkle with green onion, if using.

Makes 2 servings

# SAUTÉED SHRIMP WITH LIME AND MASCARPONE SAUCE

*This delectable dish will take mere minutes to cook if you have all the ingredients ready by the stove. Tangy lime, smoky mesquite and mellow mascarpone - pure pleasure!*

| | |
|---|---|
| 2 tbsp / 30 mL | vegetable oil |
| 1 | shallot, minced |
| 4 | garlic cloves, minced |
| 1 lb / 500 g | medium or large raw shrimp, peeled |
| ¼ tsp / 1 mL | ground paprika |
| ¼ tsp / 1 mL | mesquite seasoning |
| 2 tsp / 10 mL | granulated sugar |
| | salt and pepper, to taste |
| | juice of 2 limes |
| 2 tbsp / 30 mL | mascarpone cheese OR regular cream cheese |
| 1 tbsp / 15 mL | chopped cilantro |

Heat oil in a wok over high heat. Add shallot, garlic and shrimp. Sprinkle with paprika, mesquite seasoning, sugar, salt and pepper. Sauté shrimp 1 to 2 minutes, until pink. Stir in lime juice and mascarpone cheese; heat through. Adjust seasonings. Serve over buttered noodles or rice. Sprinkle with cilantro.

Makes 3 generous servings

# SHRIMP AND EGGPLANT STIR-FRY

*A succulent dish, ready in 30 minutes. A feast for the health-conscious gourmet.*

| | |
|---|---|
| 2 tbsp / 30 mL | vegetable oil |
| 2 | small Italian eggplants, cut into bite-sized pieces |
| 1/2 | medium sweet onion, thinly sliced |
| 24 | large raw shrimp, peeled |
| 3 | garlic cloves, minced |
| 1 | medium tomato, coarsely chopped |
| 2 tsp / 10 mL | soy sauce |
| 1/4 cup / 60 mL | spicy ketchup OR regular ketchup plus hot sauce, to taste |
| 1/4 cup / 60 mL | dry white wine |
| generous pinch | EACH, dried oregano, coriander, fennel and basil |

Heat oil in a large wok over high heat. Add eggplant and onion and stir-fry about 3 minutes. Using a spatula, push eggplant mixture to the side. Add shrimp and garlic to wok and stir-fry 2 minutes. Stir in remaining ingredients. Reduce heat to medium and cook another 2 minutes, or until heated through. Adjust seasonings. Serve immediately with rice noodles or couscous.

Makes 4 servings

*Variations: To stretch the shrimp (or other seafood), stir-fry some bite-sized cubes of extra-firm tofu along with the shrimp. It's delicious, healthy and less expensive.*

# SHRIMP AND CHICKEN PAELLA

*Paella (pi-Ay-yuh) is one of the most renowned dishes of Spanish cuisine. Originally from the Valencia region, it was named for the broad, shallow two-handled pan (paella) it was cooked in. Paella is a hearty nutritious dish with lots of colorful and flavorful ingredients — all cooked together in one pot. It can be made ahead and reheated.*

| | |
|---|---|
| 4 | chicken legs |
| 4 | chicken thighs |
| | salt and pepper, to taste |
| 1 tbsp / 15 mL | vegetable oil |
| 1 | medium onion, chopped |
| 2-3 | garlic cloves, minced |
| 4 | medium mushrooms, quartered |
| 1 | green OR red bell pepper, chopped |
| 1 cup / 250 mL | short-grain rice |
| 14 oz / 398 mL | can stewed tomatoes |
| 1 cup / 250 mL | chicken broth |
| several shakes | hot red chili flakes |
| ½ tsp / 1 mL | ground allspice |
| 14 oz / 398 mL | can chickpeas, drained and rinsed |
| 12 | pitted black Spanish OR kalamata olives |
| 8 | cherry tomatoes, halved |
| 12 | medium raw shrimp, peeled |
| 2 tbsp / 30 mL | chopped fresh parsley |

Sprinkle chicken with salt and pepper. Heat oil in a large saucepan over medium-high heat. Add chicken and brown, about 2 minutes per side.

Add onion, garlic, mushrooms and peppers and sauté 2 to 3 minutes. Stir in rice, stewed tomatoes, chicken broth, chili flakes and allspice.

Bring to a boil. Cover, reduce heat to low and simmer 20 minutes, or until most of the liquid is absorbed. If mixture is dry, add a little broth.

Fold in chickpeas, olives, tomatoes, shrimp and parsley. Cover and simmer 6 to 8 minutes, until shrimp are pink and rice is tender. Adjust seasonings. To reheat, add a little broth.

Makes 4 to 6 servings

**Variations**: *Add 12 scrubbed mussels with the shrimp. Replace 2 chicken legs with 1 cup (250 mL) diced chorizo (spicy Spanish sausage). Stir in 6 to 8 saffron threads.*

# MARINATED GRILLED BABY SQUID

*Cleaned, frozen baby squid (calamari) are easy to find in most supermarkets. They are inexpensive and taste delicious when marinated in a citrus-based sauce, then grilled very briefly over a hot fire.*

| 2 lbs / 1 kg | cleaned baby squid, fresh or frozen (thawed) |

**Citrus and Mint Marinade:**

| ¼ cup / 60 mL | EACH, fresh lemon, lime and orange juice |
| ¼ cup / 60 mL | olive oil |
| small handful | fresh mint leaves, finely chopped |
| 1 tsp / 5 mL | Maggi Seasoning OR soy sauce |
| | salt and pepper, to taste |

| ¼ cup / 60 mL | bread crumbs (optional) |

Place squid in a large rimmed dish.

*To make the marinade*, combine all marinade ingredients in a small bowl. Pour over squid and let marinate 10 to 15 minutes.

Grill squid over high heat for about 2 minutes per side (no longer than 2½ minutes as over-cooking results in a tough texture), basting with the marinade and sprinkling with the breadcrumbs, if using. Serve immediately with your favorite salsa or Red Onion and Tomato Salsa, page 94.

Makes 6 servings

*Pleasures*

# MEATS – POULTRY, BEEF, LAMB & PORK

# GRILLED HERBED CHICKEN BREASTS

*Fresh basil adds a distinctive flavor to this dish but dried works, too. Or, just improvise, using your favorite herbs.*

| | |
|---|---|
| 4 | medium boneless skinless chicken breast halves |
| | salt and pepper, to taste |

**Herbed Garlic Marinade:**

| | |
|---|---|
| 2 tbsp / 30 mL | chopped fresh basil |
| 3 | garlic cloves, minced |
| 1/4 tsp / 1 mL | EACH, ground coriander, dried thyme and red chili flakes |
| 2 tbsp / 30 mL | olive oil |
| 1/4 cup / 60 mL | dry white wine |

Sprinkle chicken breasts with salt and pepper and place them in a single layer in a shallow, rimmed dish.

*To make the marinade*, combine marinade ingredients in a small bowl and spoon half over chicken. Turn chicken and spoon remaining marinade over it. Cover and let marinate 1 to 2 hours.

Grill chicken on a medium-hot barbecue 3 to 4 minutes per side, or until opaque throughout. Baste with marinade during cooking. Serve over rice with your favorite salsa, such as Mango and Tomato Salsa, page 94, or try it in a sandwich or wrap.

Makes 4 servings

*Tip:* For a more uniform thickness, slightly flatten chicken breasts with a rubber mallet before sprinkling with salt and pepper.

# SWEET 'N' SOUR CHICKEN STIR-FRY

*This is one of my favorite stir-fry dishes. Quick and easy to prepare, it tastes delicious and is loaded with anti-oxidants, vitamins and fiber. You can add other vegetables, if you like, such as broccoli, carrots and celery, or make it completely vegan by substituting protein-rich tofu for the chicken. Alternatively, you may prefer beef or pork. All you need to do is make the sweet and sour sauce, then improvise with the other ingredients. A no-fail recipe every time.*

## Sweet 'n' Sour Sauce:

| | |
|---|---|
| 1/3 cup / 75 mL | white vinegar |
| 1/2 cup / 125 mL | brown sugar |
| 1/2 cup / 125 mL | ketchup |
| 1 cup / 250 mL | pineapple juice |
| 1 tbsp / 15 mL | cornstarch |
| | |
| 3 tbsp / 45 mL | vegetable oil, divided |
| 1 lb / 500 g | skinless, boneless chicken breasts, cut into 2"/5 cm strips |
| | salt and pepper, to taste |
| 1 | Spanish onion, cut into bite-sized chunks |
| 3 | garlic cloves, minced |
| 1 | red bell pepper, cut into strips |
| 1/3 cup / 75 mL | whole almonds |
| 1 cup / 250 mL | fresh bite-sized pineapple chunks |
| 8 oz / 250 mL | can water chestnuts, rinsed, drained and thinly sliced |
| 4 oz / 125 g | snow peas, ends trimmed |

**To make the sauce**, combine all sauce ingredients in a medium saucepan. Cook over medium heat, stirring until mixture thickens and comes to a boil. Set aside.

In a large wok, heat half of oil over high heat. Add chicken; sprinkle with salt and pepper. Stir-fry chicken 3 to 4 minutes, then transfer to a plate.

Pour remaining oil into wok. Add onion, garlic, peppers and almonds. Stir-fry about 5 minutes, or until starting to brown. Fold in pineapple, water chestnuts, chicken and snow peas. Stir in sauce. Return to a boil. Reduce heat to medium and cook about 3 minutes. Adjust seasonings. Serve over rice or couscous.

Makes 4 to 6 servings

# TANDOORI CHICKEN KEBABS
# WITH YOGURT CUCUMBER DIP (RAITA)

*If you're looking for a new chicken recipe, I highly recommend this one. Very flavorful, very pleasurable! You can make the marinade and dip a day ahead.*

## Tandoori Marinade:

| | |
|---|---|
| 1 cup / 250 mL | plain yogurt |
| 1/4 cup / 60 mL | olive oil |
| 1/4 cup / 60 mL | fresh lemon juice |
| 4 | garlic cloves, minced |
| 2 tsp / 10 mL | EACH, ground cumin, paprika, turmeric, sugar and salt |
| 1/2 tsp / 2 mL | EACH, ground allspice and ginger |

## Yogurt Cucumber Dip:

| | |
|---|---|
| 1/2 | medium sweet onion, coarsely chopped |
| 1 | garlic clove |
| 1/2 | seedless cucumber, thickly sliced |
| handful | fresh cilantro |
| 3/4 cup / 175 mL | plain yogurt |
| | salt and pepper, to taste |
| | |
| 10, 12" / 30 cm | wooden skewers |
| 2 lbs / 1 kg | boneless skinless chicken breasts |

*To make the marinade*, combine all marinade ingredients in a medium bowl. Cover and refrigerate until ready to use, up to 1 day.

*To make the dip*, finely chop onion, garlic, cucumber and cilantro in a chopper or blender. Transfer to a medium bowl. Stir in yogurt, salt and pepper. Cover and refrigerate until serving, up to 1 day.

Soak skewers in water for 15 minutes. Meanwhile, cut chicken breasts into 1" (2.5 cm) cubes. Thread 4 or 5 cubes onto each skewer. Place skewers in a large rimmed dish. Spoon half of marinade over chicken; turn skewers and spoon over remaining marinade. Cover and refrigerate 6 hours to overnight.

Cook chicken skewers on medium-hot grill about 7 minutes per side, or until chicken is cooked through. Serve with Yogurt Cucumber Dip.

Makes 4 to 5 servings

*Pictured on page 121.*

# CHICKEN KEBABS WITH COCONUT, GINGER AND PEANUT SAUCE

*It seems that some flavors are just meant to go together. In this distinctive sauce coconut, lime, ginger and peanut butter richly flavor the chicken while keeping it moist and tender.*

**Coconut, Ginger and Peanut Sauce:**

| | |
|---|---|
| 1 cup / 250 mL | coconut milk |
| 1/4 cup / 60 mL | fresh lime juice |
| | grated zest of 1 lime |
| 3 tbsp / 45 mL | peanut butter |
| 2 tbsp / 30 mL | honey |
| 1 tbsp / 15 mL | grated fresh ginger |
| 4-5 | garlic cloves, crushed |
| 1 tsp / 5 mL | EACH, ground cumin and coriander |
| 1/2 tsp / 2 mL | EACH, ground paprika, turmeric and allspice |
| generous pinch | EACH, salt and cayenne pepper |
| | |
| 10, 12" / 30 cm | wooden skewers |
| 2 lbs / 1 kg | boneless skinless chicken breasts |

*To make the sauce*, combine all sauce ingredients in a small saucepan. Heat over medium heat, stirring until peanut butter has melted and sauce is smooth. Cover and let cool to room temperature. Refrigerate until ready to use, up to 3 days.

Soak skewers in water for 15 minutes. Meanwhile, cut chicken breasts into 1" (2.5 cm) cubes. Thread 4 or 5 cubes onto each skewer. Place skewers in a large rimmed dish. Sprinkle with salt and pepper.

Divide sauce equally among 3 small bowls. Cover and refrigerate 2 of the bowls. Spoon sauce in third bowl over chicken, coating both sides. Cover and refrigerate 3 hours to overnight.

Cook chicken skewers on medium-hot grill about 7 minutes per side, brushing them with sauce in second bowl. Serve kebabs with rice or couscous and remaining sauce.

Makes 4 to 5 servings

# COCONUT AND CURRY CHICKEN

*A flavorful combination of Indian and Thai cuisine. To adjust the seasonings to your own taste, just use more or less turmeric, curry and allspice.*

| | |
|---|---|
| 2 tbsp / 30 mL | vegetable oil, divided |
| 8 | skinless chicken thighs |
| | salt and pepper, to taste |
| generous pinch | ground turmeric |
| 2 | garlic cloves, minced |
| 1 tbsp / 15 mL | curry powder |
| 1/2 tsp / 2 mL | ground allspice |
| 14 oz / 398 mL | can coconut milk |
| | juice and zest of 1 lemon |
| 1 1/2 tbsp / 22 mL | granulated sugar |
| 2 tbsp / 30 mL | minced sweet red pepper |
| 1 | green onion, thinly sliced |
| 4-6 | leaves fresh basil, shredded |
| 2 tbsp / 30 mL | shredded coconut |

Heat 1 tbsp (15 mL) oil in a large frying pan over high heat. Add chicken. Sprinkle with salt, pepper and turmeric. Brown both sides. Transfer to plate.

Pour remaining oil into pan. Add garlic, curry, allspice, coconut milk, lemon juice and zest, sugar and minced pepper. Season with salt and pepper. Bring to a boil.

Put chicken back in pan and cover. Reduce heat to low and simmer 15 minutes. Turn chicken over and sprinkle with green onion. Continue to simmer, uncovered, 15 to 20 minutes, occasionally spooning sauce over chicken. Just before serving, fold in basil. Adjust seasonings. Sprinkle with shredded coconut. Serve over rice or couscous.

Makes 4 servings

# BARBECUED CURRY CHICKEN

*Very easy to prepare, loaded with flavor. A busy weeknight favorite.*

| | |
|---|---|
| ¹/₂ cup / 125 mL | barbecue sauce |
| 1-2 tbsp / 15-30 mL | curry powder |
| generous pinch | EACH, dried coriander and celery salt |
| 4 | EACH, medium chicken legs and thighs |
| | salt and pepper, to taste |

In a small bowl, combine barbecue sauce, curry powder, coriander and celery salt. Set aside.

Sprinkle chicken pieces with salt and pepper. Barbecue chicken over a medium hot grill for 10 to 12 minutes per side. Brush with sauce on both sides and continue to cook 10 to 12 minutes longer.

Makes 4 servings

# STOVE-TOP QUAILS WITH MUSHROOM RICE

*A delicious meal, all in one pot. I get fresh quails at my local market but they are also available in the frozen section of some grocery stores. Quail meat has a delicate flavor and can be used in many chicken or game bird recipes.*

| | |
|---|---|
| 2 | quails, innards and necks removed |
| | salt and pepper, to taste |
| 2 | slices bacon, coarsely chopped |
| ¹/₂ cup / 125 mL | sliced mushrooms |
| 1 cup / 250 mL | Arborio rice |
| 2 cups / 500 mL | chicken broth |

Using sharp scissors, cut quails in half lengthwise. Sprinkle both sides with salt and pepper.

In a large saucepan, cook bacon for 1 minute. Add mushrooms and cook 1 more minute. Push mushrooms and bacon to one side and add quails to the saucepan, browning each side. Stir rice into mushroom/bacon mixture. Gently pour broth over rice and bring to a boil. Cover, reduce heat to low and simmer 30 to 40 minutes, or until liquid is absorbed and rice and quails are tender. Add a salad to complete the meal. Enjoy!

Makes 2 to 3 servings

# MARINATED ROAST CHICKEN

*Incredibly moist, tangy and richly flavored — and very versatile.*

| | |
|---|---|
| 3¹/₂ lb / 1.75 kg | whole chicken |

**Garlic, Lemon and White Wine Marinade:**

| | |
|---|---|
| 4 | garlic cloves, minced |
| 1 tbsp / 15 mL | EACH, hot red chili flakes, paprika and dried cilantro |
| | grated zest of 1 lemon |
| ¹/₄ cup / 60 mL | fresh lemon juice |
| ³/₄ cup / 175 mL | white wine |
| 1 tbsp / 15 mL | liquid honey |
| | salt and pepper, to taste |
| 2 tsp / 10 mL | butter |

Place chicken in a bowl or dish just large enough to hold it.

*To make the marinade*, combine marinade ingredients. Spoon marinade over chicken and into cavity. Cover and refrigerate 8 hours to overnight, turning chicken halfway through.

Preheat oven to 375°F (190°C). Drain chicken, sprinkle it with salt and pepper and place it breast side up in a roasting pan. Dot with butter. Roast 30 minutes.

Meanwhile, in a small saucepan over high heat, bring marinade to a boil. Reduce heat to low and simmer 5 minutes.

Baste chicken with marinade and continue to roast 45 minutes, basting twice.

Transfer chicken to a cutting board. Let rest 5 minutes before cutting.

Skim fat from the pan, then add pan juices to marinade in saucepan. Bring mixture to a boil and cook until thickened. Adjust seasonings. Serve with carved chicken.

Makes 4 to 5 servings

*Variation: If you want to try this very flavorful marinade with chicken breasts, marinate 3 lbs (1.5 kg) of chicken breasts (boneless, skinless, if you prefer) as above. Drain and roast as above, placing chicken breasts in a shallow pan in a single layer. Decrease roasting time to 30 to 35 minutes, basting several times. Add marinade to pan juices and thicken as above. Serve over chicken. Cold, sliced leftover chicken makes a delicious wrap, especially with leftover Mesclun, Peach and Feta Salad, page 67, added to the wrap.*

# GRILLED TURKEY BREAST WITH MANGO SALSA

*Small enough to cook on the barbecue, this little marinated roast is a pleasant change from the usual barbecue fare of hot dogs, hamburgers and steaks.*

| | |
|---|---|
| 1¹/₂-2 lb / 750 g-1 kg | boneless turkey breast, skin on |
| | salt and pepper, to taste |

**Herbed Garlic Marinade:**

| | |
|---|---|
| | juice of 1 lemon |
| 3 tbsp / 45 mL | soy sauce |
| 2-3 | garlic cloves, crushed |
| 2 tbsp / 30 mL | olive oil |
| 2 tbsp / 30 mL | chopped fresh herbs, e.g., cilantro and/or basil |

**Mango Salsa:**

| | |
|---|---|
| 1 | ripe mango, peeled, pitted and diced |
| 1 | small onion, chopped |
| 1 tbsp / 15 mL | chopped fresh mint |
| 1 tbsp / 15 mL | chopped fresh basil |
| 2 tbsp / 30 mL | balsamic vinegar, or to taste |
| 1 tsp / 5 mL | sesame oil |
| few drops | hot sauce |
| | salt, to taste |

Using string, tie turkey breast into an oval-shaped roast. Sprinkle with salt and pepper. Place roast skin side up in a small rimmed dish.

*To make the marinade*, combine marinade ingredients. Spoon marinade over roast. Cover and refrigerate 2 to 4 hours.

*To make the salsa*, combine Mango Salsa ingredients. Cover and chill until ready to serve.

About 1¹/₂ hours before serving, grease grill and heat barbecue to medium. Place turkey roast on hot grill. Close lid. Rotate roast and brush with marinade every 10 minutes to brown evenly. Continue to grill with lid closed for a total of 40 to 45 minutes, or until turkey is springy when pressed and a meat thermometer inserted into the center reads 170°F (77°C). Remove from grill and let rest 5 minutes.

Slice turkey and serve with Mango Salsa.

Makes 3 to 4 servings

# ROASTED TURKEY BREAST WITH SAUSAGE, PORK AND ONION STUFFING

*Do you find there are too many leftovers when you cook a whole turkey? Try this tasty turkey breast and stuffing which generously feeds 6 to 8 people and takes only 1½ hours of cooking time.*

## Sausage, Pork and Onion Stuffing:

| | |
|---|---|
| 4 | thick slices crusty white bread |
| ³/₄ cup / 175 mL | milk |
| 2 | Italian sausages, casings removed |
| ¹/₂ lb / 250 g | lean ground pork |
| 3 | eggs, beaten |
| ¹/₂ | medium onion, finely chopped |
| 1 | celery stick, finely chopped |
| 1 | medium carrot, finely chopped |
| 2 | garlic cloves, minced |
| 2 tbsp / 30 mL | chopped fresh cilantro |
| | salt and pepper, to taste |
| | |
| 2 lb / 1 kg | turkey breast, bone in, skin on |
| | salt and pepper, to taste |
| generous pinch | EACH, dried rosemary, fennel and coriander |
| 2 tsp / 10 mL | butter |

**To make the stuffing**, place bread in a large bowl; pour milk over it. Let soak 10 minutes, then break up with a fork. Gradually mix in remaining stuffing ingredients. Cover and refrigerate up to 1 day or freeze up to 2 weeks.

Preheat oven to 350°F (180°C).

Sprinkle turkey breast with salt and pepper. Place skin side up in a parchment-lined roasting pan and sprinkle with dried herbs. Dot with butter.

Roast turkey breast, uncovered, for 30 minutes. Spoon stuffing around breast and continue to roast 50 to 60 minutes, or until top of breast is browned and a meat thermometer inserted into the thickest part reads 180°F (83°C). Let rest 5 minutes, then slice thinly.

Serve with Orange Cranberry Sauce, page 91.

Makes 6 to 8 servings

# RABBIT BRAISED IN WHITE WINE SAUCE

*An irresistible melding of flavors — tender rabbit meat braised in a succulent full-bodied wine sauce. If you're not quite ready for rabbit, try this recipe using cut-up chicken. It's delicious, too!*

| | |
|---|---|
| 1 tbsp / 15 mL | olive oil |
| 2½ lb / 1.25 kg | rabbit, cut into 12 to 14 pieces* |
| | salt and pepper, to taste |
| 4 | garlic cloves, minced |
| ¾ cup / 175 mL | dry white wine |
| ½ | chicken bouillon cube |
| 2-3 | bay leaves |
| generous pinch | EACH, dried coriander, basil and cilantro |
| 1 cup / 125 mL | brown gravy, page 98, OR from store-bought mix |
| ¼ cup / 60 mL | sour cream |

Heat oil in a large saucepan over high heat. Sprinkle rabbit pieces with salt and pepper and brown both sides. Add garlic, wine, bouillon cube, bay leaves, coriander, basil and cilantro. Cover, reduce heat to low and simmer 40 to 45 minutes, turning rabbit twice.

Stir together gravy and sour cream and blend into wine sauce. Increase heat to high until sauce has thickened. Reduce heat to low, cover and continue to simmer 15 minutes. Adjust seasonings. Serve over Creamy Polenta, page 119, egg noodles or rice.

Makes 4 to 5 servings

* Ask your butcher to do this for you

# BEEF STIR-FRY WITH SPICY ORANGE SAUCE

*Don't let the long list of ingredients stop you from making this Szechuan-inspired dish. It's easy to make and tastes fantastic.*

| | |
|---|---|
| 2 tbsp / 15 mL | sesame oil, divided |
| 1 lb / 500 g | top sirloin steak, thinly sliced |
| | salt and pepper, to taste |
| 1 | medium sweet onion, chopped |
| 1/2 | red bell pepper, julienned |
| 1 tbsp / 15 mL | finely chopped jalapeño pepper |
| 1/2 cup / 125 mL | thickly sliced shiitake mushrooms |
| 2-3 | garlic cloves, minced |
| 1 tbsp / 15 mL | grated fresh ginger |
| 1/4 tsp / l mL | ground cloves |
| | grated zest of 1 orange |
| 1/2 cup / 125 mL | fresh orange juice, divided |
| 2 tbsp / 30 mL | soy sauce |
| 1/4 cup / 60 mL | sweet red pepper chili sauce |
| 8 oz / 250 g | fresh snow peas, ends trimmed |
| 2 tsp / 5 mL | cornstarch |
| 1 | seedless orange, peeled, quartered and thinly sliced |
| 1 tbsp / 15 mL | toasted sesame seeds |

In a large wok, heat 1 tbsp (15 mL) oil over high heat. When sizzling hot, add beef. Sprinkle with salt and pepper. Stir-fry 1 to 2 minutes, until just browned and still rare inside. Transfer beef to a plate.

Pour remaining oil into wok. Add onion, peppers and mushrooms and stir-fry 3 to 4 minutes. Stir in garlic, ginger, cloves, orange zest, 1/4 cup (60 mL) orange juice, soy sauce and chili sauce. Reduce heat to medium and mix in snow peas. Cook 2 minutes.

Stir 2 tsp (5 mL) cornstarch into remaining orange juice. Pour into wok and bring to a boil. Fold in beef and orange and heat through. Adjust seasonings. Sprinkle with sesame seeds. Serve over rice or rice noodles.

Makes 4 servings

*Variations: Try thinly sliced chicken breast or pork tenderloin instead of beef.*

*Pictured opposite.*

## MAIN COURSE – BEEF

*Beef Stir-Fry with Spicy Orange Sauce,* page 154

*Creamy Polenta,* page 119

# THE CLASSIC BURGER

*Can anything be more pleasurably pure and simple than a traditional juicy hamburger with all the trimmings? Because this is the simplest of recipes, I felt it belonged in this book.*

| | |
|---|---|
| 2 lbs / 1 kg | lean ground beef |
| 6 | crusty buns, split |
| 1-2 | ripe beefsteak tomatoes, sliced |
| 1 | large sweet onion, thinly sliced |
| | salt and pepper to taste |
| | mustard |
| | sweet pickle relish |
| | ketchup |
| | mayonnaise |
| 6 | slices Cheddar, provolone OR Asiago cheese |
| | shredded lettuce |
| | roasted chili peppers, thinly sliced |

Heat barbecue to medium-high. Lightly grease grates.

Shape beef into 6 burgers. Place burgers on grill and cook 4 to 6 minutes per side, or until meat is just slightly pink in the center.

Meanwhile, warm buns on grill or in oven. Serve burgers on bottom half bun and let family and friends add their own toppings.

Makes 6 hamburgers

# SPICY CHILI

*A timeless favorite. Just increase or reduce the spiciness to your liking.*

| | |
|---|---|
| 1 lb / 500 g | lean ground beef |
| 1/2 | medium onion, chopped |
| 2-3 | garlic cloves, chopped |
| 19 oz / 540 mL | can red kidney beans, rinsed and drained |
| 19 oz / 540 mL | can stewed tomatoes |
| 27 oz / 700 mL | jar tomato sauce |
| 2 | chipotle chilies, or to taste, finely chopped |
| 2-4 tbsp / 30-60 mL | ground chili powder, or to taste |
| 1 tsp / 5 mL | ground cumin |
| 2 tsp / 10 mL | brown sugar |
| generous pinch | EACH, dried oregano and parsley |
| | salt, to taste |

In a large frying pan, sauté beef and onions 3 to 5 minutes, or until evenly browned. Stir in remaining ingredients. Bring to a boil. Reduce heat to low. Cover and simmer 30 minutes. Uncover, stir, and continue to simmer 5 to 10 minutes, or until chili is of desired consistency. Adjust seasonings. Serve with your favorite chili toppings, e.g., chopped tomato, red pepper, onion, shredded cheese and sour cream.

Delicious with Creamy Polenta, page 119, or Buttermilk and Flaxseed Biscuits, page 33.

Makes 4 servings

*Variations*: Replace some or all of the kidney beans with canned mixed beans, chickpeas (garbanzo beans), great northern, pinto or black beans.

For **Turkey** or **Chicken Chili**, replace ground beef with ground turkey or chicken.

# GRILLED STEAK WITH FRESH HERB VINAIGRETTE

*A thick juicy steak is every meat lover's delight. Enhance its flavor by dressing it up with this zesty herb topping.*

**Fresh Herb Vinaigrette:**

| | |
|---|---|
| 1/2 cup / 125 mL | finely chopped parsley |
| 1 tbsp / 15 mL | EACH, finely chopped fresh thyme, oregano and sage |
| 1/2 | medium onion, finely chopped |
| 2 | garlic cloves, minced |
| | grated zest of 1 lemon |
| 2-3 tbsp / 30-45 mL | balsamic OR wine vinegar |
| 2 tbsp / 30 mL | olive oil |
| | salt and pepper, to taste |
| 4 | steaks, such as rib eye OR strip loin |
| | Steak Seasoning Mix, page 98, OR store-bought, to taste |

*To make the vinaigrette,* combine all ingredients in a small bowl.

Sprinkle steaks with steak seasoning. Cook steaks on a hot grill to desired doneness (3 to 4 minutes per side per 1"/2.5 cm of thickness for medium rare).

To serve, spoon herb vinaigrette over steaks.

# OVEN-ROASTED BEEF TENDERLOIN

*Exquisitely moist and tender. A very satisfying dish for beef afficionados.*

**Garlic Dijon Marinade:**

| | |
|---|---|
| 1 tsp / 5 mL | Steak Seasoning Mix, page 98, OR store-bought |
| 1 tbsp / 15 mL | Dijon mustard |
| 1 tbsp / 15 mL | soy sauce |
| 2 | garlic cloves, minced |
| 1 tsp / 5 mL | ground cumin |
| 2 tbsp / 15 mL | olive oil |
| | |
| 2 lb / 1 kg | beef tenderloin |

Combine marinade ingredients in a small bowl.

Place tenderloin on rack in roasting pan and brush marinade over top and sides. Cover and let marinate 1 hour at room temperature.

Preheat oven to 425°F (220°C).

Roast tenderloin to desired doneness, 40 to 45 minutes for rare, or until meat thermometer inserted into center of roast reads 140°F (60°C). For medium, roast 10 minutes longer, or to 160°F (70°C). Let roast rest 5 minutes, then carve.

Serve hot or cold with horseradish and/or Red Onion and Tomato Salsa, page 94.

Makes 4 to 5 servings

*Variations: This marinade is suitable for other cuts of beef as well as for pork.*

# PRIME RIB OF BEEF WITH CABERNET GRAVY

*You're sure to please when you serve this savory roast to your guests. A piquant mustard coating seals in moisture and tenderizes the meat.*

| | |
|---|---|
| 5-6 lb / 2.5-3 kg | prime rib roast |

**Dijon Brown Sugar Rub:**

| | |
|---|---|
| 1/4 cup / 60 mL | butter, softened |
| 2 tbsp / 30 mL | unbleached flour |
| 2 tsp / 10 mL | Steak Seasoning Mix, page 98, OR store-bought |
| 3 tbsp / 45 mL | Dijon mustard |
| 1 tbsp / 15 mL | brown sugar |
| 1 tsp / 5 mL | ground fennel seed |
| | pepper, to taste |

**Cabernet Gravy:**

| | |
|---|---|
| 1 cup / 250 mL | Brown Gravy, page 98, OR from store-bought mix |
| 2 | garlic cloves, minced |
| 1 | shallot, minced |
| 1 | bay leaf |
| 1/2 cup / 125 mL | Cabernet OR other dry red wine |

Place roast, rib-side down, in roasting pan. Combine rub ingredients and, using a knife, spread over top and sides of roast. Cover and let rest 1 hour at room temperature.

*To make the gravy*, in a small saucepan, prepare Brown Gravy. Reduce heat to low and add garlic, shallot, bay leaf and wine. Simmer 4 to 5 minutes, until thickened. Remove from heat and cover.

Preheat oven to 400°F (200°C).

Place roast, uncovered, in hot oven. Roast for 30 minutes, then reduce oven temperature to 350°F (180°C). Continue to roast for 45 to 60 minutes for rare, or until meat thermometer reads 140°F (60°C). For medium, roast 15 to 20 minutes longer, or to 160°F (70°C). Place roast on cutting board and let rest 5 minutes before slicing.

Meanwhile, skim fat from roasting pan and pour remaining juices into gravy. Bring to a boil. Remove bay leaf. Serve over sliced roast beef and mashed or smashed potatoes, such as Sweet and Savory Garlic Smashed Potatoes, page 116, if desired.

Makes 6 to 8 servings

# TEXAN-STYLE FAMILY POT ROAST

*Delicious comfort food for a cold wintry day — ultra-moist, tender beef simmered in a sweet and tangy tomato sauce.*

| | |
|---|---|
| 3-3¹/₂ lb / 1.5-1.75 kg | boneless beef inside blade pot roast |
| | salt and pepper, to taste |
| 2 tbsp / 30 mL | vegetable oil |
| 6 | medium cooking onions, peeled |
| 2, 14 oz / 398 mL | cans stewed tomatoes |
| 4 | garlic cloves, minced |
| generous pinch | EACH, dried basil, parsley and oregano |
| ¹/₃ cup / 75 mL | white vinegar |
| ¹/₃ cup / 75 mL | brown sugar |

Season roast with salt and pepper. In a large saucepan, heat oil over medium heat. Add roast and onions and brown on all sides. Add stewed tomatoes, garlic, basil, parsley, oregano and vinegar. Cover, reduce heat to low and simmer 2 hours, turning roast halfway through. Stir in sugar. Taste sauce and add more vinegar and sugar, if desired. Cover and continue to simmer 1 hour, or until tender.

Shortly before serving, transfer roast and onions to a cutting board and keep warm.

Using a hand blender, blend sauce in saucepan until smooth. Adjust seasonings. Carve roast and serve with onions and sauce. Roasted or mashed potatoes are the perfect accompaniment to this tasty dish.

Makes 6 servings

**Variations:** *Other cuts of stewing beef, such as brisket, lend themselves well to this recipe.*

# VEAL KIDNEYS IN CREAMY WINE SAUCE

*In many countries, veal kidneys are prized for their delicate flavor and firm yet tender texture. Kidneys, as well as other organ meats, are slowly finding their way into our kitchens due to the ever-increasing mosaic of ethnic markets and restaurants. Veal kidneys are inexpensive, can be deliciously prepared, and are very rich in iron.*

| | |
|---|---|
| 1½ lbs / 750 g | veal OR baby beef kidneys |
| 3 tbsp / 45 mL | vegetable oil, divided |
| ½ | medium onion, thinly sliced |
| 1 tbsp / 15 mL | unbleached flour |
| ½ cup / 125 mL | chicken OR vegetable broth |
| ¼ cup / 60 mL | dry red wine |
| 2 | bay leaves |
| generous pinch | EACH, ground coriander and oregano |
| ¼ cup / 60 mL | whipping OR half and half cream |
| | salt and pepper, to taste |

Remove fatty parts from kidneys, using a sharp knife or scissors. Slice kidneys into ½" (1.3 cm) rounds. Place in colander and rinse thoroughly under cold water.

In a medium frying pan, heat 1 tbsp (15 mL) oil over high heat. Add kidneys and sauté 1 to 2 minutes, stirring to cook evenly. Transfer to colander and rinse again under cold water.

Pour remaining oil into frying pan and heat over medium heat. Stir flour into oil until smooth. Add onion and sauté 1 or 2 minutes. Gradually stir in broth and wine and bring to a boil, stirring to smooth out any lumps. Add bay leaves, coriander and oregano.

Return kidneys to the pan. Reduce heat to low and simmer 3 to 5 minutes, or until kidneys are cooked but still pink inside. Fold in cream, salt and pepper and heat through. Serve over rice, pasta or Creamy Polenta, page 119.

Makes 4 servings

# ROAST LEG OF LAMB WITH SAUTÉED MUSHROOMS

*Always special. Always festive.*

**Herbed Rub:**

| | |
|---|---|
| 1/2 tsp / 2 mL | EACH, ground coriander, fennel, dried cilantro and Steak Seasoning Mix, page 98, OR store-bought |
| | salt and pepper, to taste |
| | |
| 2 lb / 1 kg | boneless or 3 lb (1.5 kg) bone-in leg of lamb |
| 3 | garlic cloves, crushed |

Combine rub ingredients and rub all over roast. Place in a parchment-lined baking dish. With a knife, spread crushed garlic over top and sides of roast. Cover, refrigerate and let marinate 1 to 3 hours.

Preheat oven to 400°F (200°C).

Bake boneless roast about 1 hour 15 minutes for medium rare (if using bone-in roast, bake about 20 minutes longer), or until thermometer inserted into center reads 140°F (60°C).

Transfer roast to cutting board and let sit 5 minutes. Carve roast into thin slices. Top with Sautéed Mushrooms, below.

Makes 5 to 6 servings

**Sautéed Mushrooms:**

| | |
|---|---|
| 1 tbsp / 15 mL | butter |
| 1 lb / 500 g | button OR cremini mushrooms, thinly sliced |
| 1 | shallot, minced |
| 1 | celery stalk, finely chopped |
| 1 | chicken bouillon cube, crumbled |
| generous pinch | dried tarragon |
| 1/4 cup / 60 mL | whipping cream |
| | salt and pepper, to taste |

In a large frying pan, heat butter over high heat. Add mushrooms and shallots and sauté 5 minutes, or until starting to brown. Add celery, bouillon cube and tarragon. Sauté until mushrooms are browned, about 5 minutes.

Stir in whipping cream. Reduce heat to medium and continue to cook 2 to 3 minutes, or until sauce has thickened slightly. Adjust seasonings. Serve over lamb or as an accompaniment to pork, beef or chicken.

# SPICED LAMB KOFTAS ON A STICK

*Spice up these Turkish "delights" with cumin, turmeric, allspice and cinnamon, and grill them as you would regular hamburgers. They taste fantastic on pitas with a refreshing yogurt-based dip, such as the Yogurt Cucumber Dip, page 146. For appetizer servings, use shorter skewers.*

| | |
|---|---|
| 10, 12" / 30 cm | wooden skewers |
| 2 | eggs |
| 2 | thick slices white bread |
| 2 lbs / 1 kg | ground lamb |
| 4-6 | garlic cloves, minced |
| ½ | medium onion, finely chopped |
| small handful | cilantro OR mint, finely chopped |
| 1½ tsp / 7 mL | ground cumin |
| ½ tsp / 2 mL | EACH, ground turmeric, allspice and cinnamon |
| generous pinch | cayenne pepper |
| | salt, to taste |

Soak skewers in water for 15 minutes.

Beat eggs in a medium bowl. Tear bread into small pieces and mix into egg. Let sit 5 minutes, or until bread has absorbed the egg and is soft. Beat with a fork to blend.

Place lamb in a large bowl. Using a fork or your hands, mix in egg mixture and remaining ingredients. Shape into 10 regular-sized (or 20 appetizer-sized) logs and skewer lengthwise all the way through.

Heat barbecue to medium-high. Lightly grease grates.

Gently place koftas on grill and cook 8 to 10 minutes, rotating to brown all sides.

Makes 8 main or 16 appetizer servings

*Variations:* For **Spiced Beef, Turkey or Chicken Koftas**, substitute beef or ground turkey or chicken for the lamb.

# GARLIC AND GINGER PORK KEBABS

*Pork needs a little boost from stronger, complementary flavors which enhance its natural mildness. The addition of garlic, ginger, allspice and balsamic vinegar does this beautifully.*

| | |
|---|---|
| 4, 9" / 23 cm | wooden skewers |
| 1¹/₂ lb / 750 g | pork tenderloin, cut into 1" (2.5 cm) cubes |

**Garlic Ginger Marinade:**

| | |
|---|---|
| ¹/₄ cup / 60 mL | soy sauce |
| 1 tbsp / 15 mL | grated fresh ginger |
| 2-3 | garlic cloves, minced |
| 2 tsp / 10 mL | granulated sugar |
| 2 tbsp / 30 mL | balsamic vinegar |
| ¹/₂ tsp / 2 mL | allspice |
| | pepper, to taste |

Soak skewers in water for about 15 minutes.

Thread 4 or 5 pork cubes onto each skewer. Place skewers in a single layer in a shallow rimmed dish.

In a small bowl, combine marinade ingredients and spoon over pork. Cover and chill 2 to 4 hours, turning skewers halfway through.

Grill pork over medium-high heat about 7 minutes per side, basting with remaining marinade. Serve with your favorite dip or salsa.

Makes 3 to 4 servings

# BARBECUED PORK TENDERLOINS

*These marinated and succulently "tender loins" taste terrific either hot or cold. I'm sure your friends will ask you for the recipe.*

| | |
|---|---|
| 2 | pork tenderloins (approximately 1$\frac{1}{2}$ lbs/750 g) |
| 2-3 | garlic cloves, crushed |
| 1$\frac{1}{2}$ tbsp / 22 mL | Dijon mustard |
| 1 tbsp / 15 mL | brown sugar |
| 3 tbsp / 45 mL | balsamic vinegar |
| few drops | Tabasco sauce |
| 2 tbsp / 30 mL | olive oil |
| $\frac{1}{2}$ tsp / 2 mL | ground cumin |
| generous pinch | ground coriander |

Trim tenderloins of any fat. Place in a shallow, rimmed dish just large enough to hold them.

In a small bowl, combine remaining ingredients. Spoon over tenderloins. Cover, refrigerate and let marinate 6 to 8 hours, turning tenderloins a few times and spooning marinade over them.

Barbecue tenderloins over medium heat 35 to 45 minutes, rotating them for even browning. Meat should be cooked through but slightly pink in the center. Let rest 5 minutes. Slice into $\frac{1}{2}$" (1.3 cm) rounds and serve with your favorite salsa, such as Peach and Tomato Salsa, page 90.

Makes 4 to 5 servings

# PORK ROAST WITH MUSHROOM GRAVY

*A deliciously moist pork roast for a traditional family dinner. You can't go wrong with this easy recipe.*

| | |
|---|---|
| 2 lb / 1 kg | boneless pork rib roast |
| ½ tsp / 2 mL | EACH, dried oregano, cilantro, thyme, ground cumin, paprika and fennel seed |
| | salt and pepper, to taste |
| 2-3 | garlic cloves, crushed |

**Mushroom Gravy:**

| | |
|---|---|
| 1 cup / 250 mL | Brown Gravy, page 98, OR store-bought mix |
| 2 tsp / 10 mL | vegetable oil |
| 4-6 | medium cremini OR button mushrooms, chopped |
| 1 | shallot, minced |

Place roast in a roasting pan and sprinkle all sides with herbs and spices, salt and pepper. Using a knife, spread crushed garlic over top and sides of roast. Cover and let sit at room temperature for 1 hour.

*To make the gravy*, in a medium saucepan, prepare Brown Gravy. Cover and set aside. In a medium frying pan, heat oil over high heat. Add mushrooms, and sauté until starting to brown. Add shallot and sauté 1 minute. Stir into gravy. Cover and set aside.

Place roast, uncovered, in preheated 400°F (200°C) oven. Roast for 30 minutes, then reduce oven temperature to 350°F (180°C). Continue to roast for 30 to 40 minutes, or until meat thermometer inserted into center of roast reads 150°F (65°C). Place roast on cutting board and let rest 5 minutes before slicing.

Meanwhile, skim fat from roasting pan and pour remaining juices into gravy. Bring to a boil. Serve over pork slices. Leftover pork makes delicious sandwiches.

Makes 4 to 5 servings

# SMOKED BACK RIBS

*Because this is one of my partner Chuck's recipes, I thought he should write it up. All I can say is that these ribs fulfill every rib lover's fantasies.*

| | |
|---|---|
| 2 racks | pork back ribs |
| | Barbecue Spice Rub, below, OR Steak Seasoning Mix, page 98, OR store-bought |
| | favorite barbecue sauce |

Serious rib eaters will each demand his or her own rack. If served with traditional side dishes of beans, coleslaw and potatoes, and with the ribs separated, a meaty rack is sufficient for two people.

Preheat oven to 200°F (93°C).

Rub the dry rub into the meat. Wrap each rack in aluminum foil and bake for 4 hours.

In the last hour, prepare wood chips and the barbecue as for Apple Wood-Smoked Salmon, page 128. When the barbecue is ready, remove the ribs from the oven and from the foil and place meat-side-up on the side of the grill, furthest from the charcoal. Specially designed rib racks, which hold the ribs vertically on edge, are widely available. These permit more ribs to be cooked simultaneously.

Cook in the same manner as the Apple Wood-Smoked Salmon, for about 1 hour 15 minutes. While there is no need to turn the ribs, if flat on the grill, it may be necessary to rearrange them once or twice when adding wood chips so that all racks cook at the same speed.

In the last 10 minutes, brush with barbecue sauce 2 or 3 times.

Makes 2 to 4 servings

# BARBECUE SPICE RUB

| | |
|---|---|
| 2 tbsp / 30 mL | paprika |
| 2 tsp / 10 mL | EACH, red pepper flakes, celery seeds, brown sugar and salt |
| 1 tsp / 5 mL | EACH, ground cumin, ground coriander and garlic powder |

Combine all ingredients. Generously sprinkle ribs with rub. Store remaining rub in an airtight container and refrigerate up to 2 months.

# GRILLED HAM STEAK WITH SPICY APRICOT SALSA

*Five minutes on a hot grill is all it takes to transform a simple slice of ham into a succulent steak. Spice it up with this hot, sweet and tangy Spicy Apricot Salsa.*

**Spicy Apricot Salsa:**

| | |
|---|---|
| 8 | ripe apricots, pitted and diced |
| 1/4 cup / 60 mL | chopped fresh basil |
| 1 | jalapeño chile, seeded and minced |
| 1 | green onion, thinly sliced |
| 2 tbsp / 30 mL | apricot jam |
| 2 tbsp / 30 mL | fresh lime OR lemon juice |
| pinch | salt |
| | |
| 1 1/2 lb / 750 g | cooked center-cut ham steak, about 1/2"/1.3 cm thick |
| 1 tbsp / 15 mL | vegetable oil |

*To prepare the salsa*, combine all salsa ingredients. Cover and refrigerate until ready to serve, up to 2 days.

Brush ham on both sides with oil. Place ham on hot barbecue grill and cook for about 5 minutes, turning once for even browning. Serve with salsa.

Makes 4 servings

*Variations*: Serve **Spicy Apricot Salsa** *with grilled or roasted chicken breasts or pork tenderloin or chops.*

# CHOUCROUTE GARNIE (Sauerkraut with Smoked Pork Hocks, Chops and Sausages)

*Strasbourg, in Alsace-Lorraine, France, is the place to go if you want to taste the best sauerkraut in the world. There, rushing from table to table, waiters balance steaming platters of this fermented cabbage piled high with different kinds of smoked meats and sausage. This local specialty is a feast for the palate, eyes and nose.*

*But there's no need to travel to Strasbourg in your quest for authentic sauerkraut; you can prepare it very easily in your own kitchen. My mother cooks it several times during the winter, regaling the whole family with this most flavorful of comfort foods. Be sure to make a big potful — sauerkraut gets better every time you warm it up.*

| | |
|---|---|
| 2 lbs / 1 kg | canned sauerkraut |
| 4 | strips bacon, chopped |
| 2 cups / 500 mL | dry white wine |
| 1/4 tsp / 1 mL | caraway seeds |
| 6-8 | juniper berries (optional) |
| 1 | smoked pork hock (ham hock, pig's feet or trotters) |
| 1 | medium potato, peeled and grated |
| 3 | smoked pork chops |
| 6 | Frankfurter sausages |

Drain sauerkraut and rinse under cold water. Squeeze out excess moisture with a paper towel.

In a large non-corrosive saucepan, over medium heat, fry bacon for 2 to 3 minutes. Add sauerkraut and cook another 2 to 3 minutes while separating the strands with a fork. Stir in wine, caraway seeds and juniper berries, if using. Bring to a boil.

Make a well in the center of the sauerkraut and place the pork hock in it. Cover, reduce heat to low and simmer for about 1 hour, stirring occasionally and adding a little wine or water, as needed, to keep the sauerkraut moist.

Fold potato into sauerkraut. Top with chops and sausages and simmer 1/2 hour.

Cut meats into serving portions. Transfer sauerkraut to a large platter and garnish with meats. Serve with boiled potatoes.

Makes 6 to 8 servings

# CABBAGE LASAGNE

*Many of us enjoy cabbage rolls but few of us would ever consider making them from scratch. It's far too labor intensive! You may want to try this shortcut version though; you simply layer the cabbage and stuffing and bake it in the oven like lasagne.*

| 1 | medium cabbage |
|---|---|

**Beef, Veal and Bratwurst Stuffing:**

| 2 lbs / 1 kg | lean ground beef |
|---|---|
| 1/2 lb / 250 g | ground veal OR chicken |
| 2 | bratwurst OR country-style sausages, casings removed |
| 1 cup / 250 mL | cooked rice |
| 2 tbsp / 30 mL | tomato paste |
| 2 | eggs, beaten |
| 1/4 cup / 60 mL | chopped fresh parsley |
| 1/2 | medium onion, chopped |
| 2 | garlic cloves, minced |
| | salt and pepper, to taste |
| 28 oz / 796 mL | can stewed tomatoes, divided |

Cut cabbage in half lengthwise and remove and discard core. Loosen leaves as much as possible. Steam cabbage (or boil in 1 cup (250 mL) water) until wilted and tender-crisp, 10 to 15 minutes for the cabbage center, less for the loosened leaves.

**To make the stuffing,** using a fork or your hands, combine stuffing ingredients in a large bowl.

Spread about 1/3 of the stewed tomatoes over bottom of a greased lasagne baking dish. Cover with half the cabbage leaves. Spread stuffing evenly over cabbage. Cover with remaining cabbage, gently pressing down to flatten and reduce air pockets. Top with remaining stewed tomatoes.

Loosely cover with foil and bake at 350°F (180°C) about 1 hour 15 minutes.

Makes 8 servings

## DESSERTS

*Lemon Cream Phyllo Cups with Strawberry Coulis,* page 178

*Lemon Cream with fresh berries,* page 178

# Pleasures

# DESSERTS

# CREAMY DIP FOR FRESH FRUIT

*A little lighter than pure whipped cream, this dip tastes like crème fraiche and takes just a few minutes to prepare.*

| | |
|---|---|
| 1/3 cup / 75 mL | whipping cream |
| 1 tbsp / 15 mL | granulated sugar |
| 1/3 cup / 75 mL | EACH, sour cream and plain yogurt |

In a medium bowl, whip cream and sugar until stiff. Add sour cream and yogurt and blend until smooth.

Makes 1 cup (250 mL)

*Variations:* For a **Chocolate Dip**, *blend 1 tbsp (15 mL) unsweetened cocoa into the plain dip.*

For a **Strawberry Dip**, *substitute 1/3 cup (75 mL) puréed strawberries for the sour cream or yogurt in the plain dip.*

For a **Liqueur Dip**, *blend 1 to 2 tbsp (15 to 30 mL) Cointreau or Grand Marnier, amaretto, Kahlúa or Tia Maria, etc. into the plain dip.*

# FROZEN BANANAS WITH CHOCOLATE KAHLÚA SAUCE

*Bananas and chocolate … two aphrodisiacs in one simple dessert … pure pleasure!*

| | |
|---|---|
| 2 | bananas, peeled and sliced |

**Chocolate Kahlúa Sauce:**

| | |
|---|---|
| 2 oz / 55 g | semisweet chocolate, chopped |
| 1/4 cup / 60 mL | whipping cream |
| 1-2 tbsp / 15-30 mL | Kahlúa OR other coffee-flavored liqueur |

Place banana slices in a single layer on a parchment-lined tray. Cover and freeze 3 hours to 1 week.

*To make the sauce*, place chocolate in a microwavable bowl. Pour cream over it. Microwave on high for 1 minute. Add Kahlúa and stir until smooth.

To serve, dip frozen banana slices into warm sauce.

Makes 3 to 4 servings

# BANANAS BRAISED IN COCONUT MILK AND GRAND MARNIER

*Some pleasures are pure and simple while others, like this one, are exquisitely sinful. One of my favorite desserts.*

| | |
|---|---|
| 1 cup / 250 mL | coconut milk |
| | juice of 1 lime |
| 2 tbsp / 30 mL | Grand Marnier |
| 4 tbsp / 60 mL | brown sugar, divided |
| 2 tbsp / 30 mL | butter |
| 4 | ripe but firm bananas, peeled and halved lengthwise |
| 1/4 cup / 60 mL | chocolate shavings |

In a small bowl, stir together coconut milk, lime juice, Grand Marnier and 2 tbsp (30 mL) sugar. Set aside.

In a large saucepan, melt butter over medium heat. Add bananas and sprinkle them with 1 tbsp (15 mL) sugar. Cook 4 to 5 minutes, or until lightly browned; turn over and sprinkle with remaining sugar. Gently pour half of coconut mixture into pan. Bring to a boil. Reduce heat to low and simmer 3 to 4 minutes, or until sauce has thickened slightly. Add remaining coconut mixture and return to a boil.

With a spatula, transfer 2 banana halves to each plate. Spoon sauce over bananas; sprinkle with chocolate shavings. Serve warm.

Makes 4 servings

# LEMON CREAM PHYLLO CUPS
# WITH STRAWBERRY COULIS

*Sophisticated, dazzling and light, this delectable dessert is the perfect ending to an elegant dinner. The crisp phyllo cups can be made 3 to 4 days ahead.*

**Phyllo Cups:**

| | |
|---|---|
| 2 | sheets phyllo pastry |
| 2 tbsp / 30 mL | butter, melted, divided |
| 1 tbsp / 15 mL | granulated sugar, divided |

**Strawberry Coulis:**

| | |
|---|---|
| 2 cups / 500 mL | strawberries OR raspberries, fresh or frozen |
| 1/2 cup / 125 mL | granulated sugar |

**Lemon Cream:**

| | |
|---|---|
| 1 cup / 250 mL | whipping cream |
| 1/4 cup / 60 mL | granulated sugar |
| 1/2 cup / 125 mL | cream cheese, softened |
| 1/4 cup / 60 mL | fresh lemon juice |
| | grated zest of 1 lemon |

*To make the phyllo cups*, cut 2 phyllo sheets in half. Place a half sheet on work surface; brush with a little butter and sprinkle with a little sugar. Repeat with remaining 3 half sheets, stacking them into 4 layers. Using scissors, cut stack into 6 equal squares. Lightly press phyllo squares into 6 greased muffin tins, leaving the uneven edges upright. Prick bottoms with fork.

Bake at 350°F (180°C) for about 8 minutes, or until lightly browned. Let cool 5 minutes, then remove from tins and let cool completely on wire rack. If making ahead, store in an airtight container up to 4 days.

*To make the coulis*, blend strawberries and sugar in blender until smooth. Cover; refrigerate up to 2 days.

*To make the cream*, whip cream and sugar in a medium bowl until stiff. In a small bowl, using the same beaters, blend cream cheese with lemon juice. Add zest. Fold into whipped cream. Cover; refrigerate up to 6 hours.

Just before serving, spoon Lemon Cream into cups and drizzle with coulis. Drizzle more coulis on plates around each cup.

Makes 6 servings

*Variation*: Don't have time to make the Phyllo Cups? Just serve the Lemon Cream in wine or parfait glasses and top with the coulis and/or fresh berries.

Pictured on page 173.

# BERRY TRIFLE

*Traditional yet trendy, a colorful well-assembled trifle is always in style. This classic English dessert is easy to make if you use the store-bought custard and ladyfingers called for in the following recipe. Take care, though, to assemble the trifle in the order given so that the ladyfingers can soak up the strawberry sauce and custard.*

| 4 cups / 1 L | strawberries, fresh or frozen |
|---|---|
| 1/2 cup / 125 mL | granulated sugar |
| 2, 3 oz / 85 g | packages ladyfingers |
| 2, 8 oz / 250 g | cans English Devon-style custard |
| 3/4 cup / 175 mL | EACH, fresh raspberries and blueberries, reserving a few for garnish |
| 1 cup / 250 mL | whipping cream |
| 2 tbsp / 30 mL | granulated sugar |

In a blender, purée strawberries with 1/2 cup (125 mL) sugar. Transfer to a bowl, cover and refrigerate up to 2 days.

Pour half of puréed strawberries into bottom of a large deep glass bowl. Place half of ladyfingers in a single layer on top. Spoon half of custard over ladyfingers. Sprinkle with half of berries. Repeat with 1 more layer, ending with berries. Cover and refrigerate 6 hours to overnight.

Up to 3 hours before serving, whip cream with 2 tbsp (30 mL) sugar. Spread over trifle. Garnish with remaining berries.

Makes 8 to 10 servings

*Variations*: Sprinkle ladyfingers with 2 to 4 tbsp (30 to 60 mL) sherry, brandy or rum before topping them with custard. Add grated or shaved chocolate to the berry garnish and/or 2 tbsp (30 mL) toasted, slivered almonds.

# OLD-FASHIONED RICE PUDDING

*"Simply delicious" is how I'd describe this traditional rice pudding. Young and old, and everyone in-between, will enjoy this comforting dessert. If you like, dress it up with berries, chopped fruit or candied ginger or spoon over some chocolate sauce or maple syrup.*

| | |
|---|---|
| 2½ cups / 625 mL | milk |
| 1 or 2 | cinnamon sticks |
| 1 cup / 250 mL | Arborio rice |
| ⅓ cup / 75 mL | raisins |
| ¼ cup / 60 mL | granulated sugar |
| ¼ cup / 60 mL | whipping OR half-and-half cream |

In a medium saucepan, over medium-high heat, bring milk to a boil. Add cinnamon sticks and rice. Return to a boil, cover and reduce heat to low. Simmer for 35 minutes, stirring occasionally and adding a little milk if rice is dry.

Fold in raisins, sugar and cream and simmer another 10 to 15 minutes, or until rice is tender and pudding is creamy. Serve warm or cold.

Makes 4 to 5 servings

*Variations:* For a **Grand Marnier Rice Pudding** or a **Rum Raisin Rice Pudding**, marinate raisins in 2 tbsp (30 mL) of Grand Marnier or rum for at least an hour before adding to pudding. You can also add 1 tsp (5 mL) of vanilla and a dash of nutmeg.

# CHOCOLATE-STUFFED FIGS

*A gourmet dessert — plump figs that have been simmered in sweet honey and Marsala wine, topped with a little melted chocolate. Divine!*

| | |
|---|---|
| 12 | large dried figs |
| 1/2 cup / 125 mL | EACH, liquid honey, Marsala wine and water |
| 2 tbsp / 30 mL | semisweet chocolate chips |

Place figs in a medium saucepan. Pour honey, wine and water over them. Bring to a boil, cover, reduce heat to low and simmer 15 minutes. Remove from heat and let sit 3 hours to overnight.

Drain figs, reserving liquid. Transfer figs to a microwavable platter, stem side up. Snip off stems with scissors and stuff each fig with a few chocolate chips. Reheat honey Marsala liquid and let boil 3 to 5 minutes, or until slightly thickened. Pour over figs. (Can be made 1 day ahead.)

Just before serving, heat figs in microwave oven for 1 to 2 minutes, or until chocolate has melted. Serve with a dollop of whipped cream, sour cream or yogurt, if desired.

Makes 6 servings

# CARAMELIZED APPLE SLICES

*The thinner the apple slices, the better they'll taste. Serve them warm or cold, either as a light dessert, topped with a dollop of whipped cream or ice cream, as a filling or topping for Buckwheat Crêpes, page 10, or Buttermilk Apple Pancakes, page 11, or as an accompaniment to chicken, turkey or pork. Pleasure couldn't be any simpler!*

| | |
|---|---|
| 4-5 | medium apples (such as Fuji, Gala, Golden Delicious, Granny Smith or Mutsu), peeled, cored and thinly sliced with a mandolin |
| 2 tbsp / 30 mL | butter, melted |
| 2-3 tbsp / 30-45 mL | granulated sugar (depending on tartness of apples), divided |
| 1/4 tsp / 1 mL | ground cinnamon |

Preheat oven to 400°F (200°C). In a large bowl, toss apples with butter, 2 tbsp (30 mL) sugar and cinnamon. Spread evenly in a 9 x 13" (23 x 33 cm) baking dish. Sprinkle with remaining sugar. Bake 20 to 25 minutes.

Makes 4 dessert or 8 side servings

# LEMON CAKE SQUARES

*Over the years, I've tried several versions of these light, sponge cake-like squares. This one seems to be everybody's favorite.*

| | |
|---|---|
| 1/4 cup / 60 mL | butter OR margarine, softened |
| 1/2 cup / 125 mL | granulated sugar |
| 1/2 cup / 125 mL | plain yogurt |
| 1 | egg |
| | grated zest of 1/2 lemon |
| 1/4 cup / 60 mL | fresh lemon juice |
| 1 cup / 250 mL | unbleached flour |
| 2 tsp / 10 mL | baking powder |

Preheat oven to 350°F (180°C). Lightly grease a 9" (23 cm) square baking dish.

In a medium bowl, beat together butter and sugar. Beat in yogurt, egg, lemon peel and juice. Stir in flour and baking powder. Spread batter evenly in baking dish.

Bake 25 to 30 minutes, or until toothpick inserted in center comes out clean. When cool, spread Lemon Glaze (below) over top of cake. Cut into squares.

**Lemon Glaze:**

| | |
|---|---|
| 2/3 cup / 150 mL | icing (confectioner's) sugar |
| | grated zest of 1/2 lemon |
| 1 1/2 tbsp / 22 mL | lemon juice |

In a small bowl, using a fork, mix all ingredients to a spreading consistency.

Makes 12 squares

*Variation*: For **Lemon Cupcakes**, line 9 regular or 18 small-sized muffin pans with paper cups. Divide batter among them and bake about 20 minutes. When cool drizzle with Lemon Glaze, above, or frost with Lemon Cream, page 178, or your favorite frosting.

# STRAWBERRY PUDDING CAKE

*The fragrant perfume of freshly baked strawberries makes this simple low-fat dessert very appealing.*

| | |
|---|---|
| 1 cup / 250 mL | plain yogurt |
| 1 tsp / 5 mL | baking soda |
| 1/2-3/4 cup / 125-175 mL | granulated sugar, depending on tartness of berries |
| 4 tsp / 20 mL | unsalted butter, melted, divided |
| 1 cup / 250 mL | unbleached flour |
| pinch | salt |
| 2 1/2 cups / 625 mL | sliced strawberries |
| 2 tbsp / 30 mL | sliced or slivered almonds |
| 2 tbsp / 30 mL | brown sugar |

Preheat oven to 350°F (180°C). Grease an 8" (20 cm) square baking dish.

In a medium bowl, stir together yogurt, baking soda, sugar and half of butter. Mix in flour and salt until just combined. Fold in strawberries and spread batter evenly in baking dish. Top with almonds and brown sugar. Sprinkle with remaining butter.

Bake 30 to 35 minutes, or until pudding is nicely browned and puffed.

Spoon onto plates while warm or cut into squares when cold. Serve with whipped cream or ice cream.

Makes 6 to 8 servings

# CHERRY CLAFOUTI

*Often, I find, the simplest is the best. To make this delicious crustless pie, just mix all the ingredients together to form a thick batter. Spoon half of it into a pie plate, spread cherries over it and top with the remaining batter. Voilà! Pleasure, pure and simple ...*

| | |
|---|---|
| 1½ cups / 375 mL | pitted bing cherries, canned or frozen |
| ½ cup / 125 mL | unsalted butter, softened |
| 1 cup / 250 mL | granulated sugar |
| 2 | eggs |
| 1 cup / 250 mL | plain yogurt |
| ¼ cup / 60 mL | fresh lemon juice |
| | grated zest of 1 lemon |
| 1 cup / 250 mL | unbleached flour |
| ¼ cup / 60 mL | ground almonds |
| 1 tsp / 5 mL | baking powder |
| pinch | salt |
| 2 tbsp / 30 mL | slivered almonds |
| 1 tbsp / 15 mL | brown sugar |

Preheat oven to 350°F (180°C). Lightly grease a 9" (23 cm) pie plate. Drain cherries. Set aside.

Using a fork or electric mixer, cream butter and sugar in a medium bowl. Mix in eggs, yogurt, lemon juice and zest. Fold in flour, almonds, baking powder and salt to form a thick batter. Spoon half of batter evenly into prepared pie plate. Spread cherries evenly over batter, then top with remaining batter. Sprinkle with almonds and brown sugar.

Bake 50 to 60 minutes, or until lightly browned and a toothpick inserted in center comes out clean. Serve warm or at room temperature.

Makes 8 servings

***Variations***: Although the classic clafouti recipe uses cherries, you can substitute chopped apples, pears, peaches or plums for the cherries.

# BLUEBERRY PIE

*Lemon transforms the mellow sweetness of blueberries from the merely delicious to the sublime. A heavenly experience.*

**Sweet Pastry Crust:**

| | |
|---|---|
| 1 cup / 250 mL | unbleached flour |
| 1/4 cup / 60 mL | granulated sugar |
| pinch | salt |
| 1 tsp / 5 mL | baking powder |
| 1/2 cup / 125 mL | butter OR margarine, chilled |
| 1/4 cup / 60 mL | sliced almonds, toasted |
| 1 | large egg, beaten |

**Blueberry Filling:**

| | |
|---|---|
| 4 cups / 1 L | fresh blueberries |
| 1/4 cup / 60 mL | granulated sugar |
| 1 tbsp / 15 mL | grated lemon zest |
| 1/4 cup / 60 mL | fresh lemon juice |
| 5 tsp / 25 mL | unbleached flour |
| 1 tbsp / 15 mL | butter OR margarine, melted |

**Topping:**

| | |
|---|---|
| 1 tsp / 5 mL | milk |
| 2 tsp / 10 mL | granulated sugar |

Preheat oven to 350°F (180°C).

*To make the pastry*, combine flour, sugar, salt and baking powder in a medium bowl. Cut butter into flour with a pastry cutter until mixture resembles coarse crumbs. Fold in almonds. Work in egg until dough holds together. Press 3/4 of dough firmly and evenly against bottom and sides of an ungreased 9" (23 cm) pie plate. On a floured surface, roll out remaining dough to 1/4" (6 mm) thickness and cut out different shapes with a small cookie cutter (e.g., leaves or stars).

*To make the filling*, pour blueberries into a large bowl. Fold in remaining filling ingredients. Spoon berry mixture into pie shell. Garnish with dough cut-outs. Brush cut-outs with milk and sprinkle with a little sugar.

Bake for 50 minutes, or until crust is golden and berries are juicy and bubbly. If crust turns brown before berries release their juices, loosely cover pie with aluminum foil and continue to bake until done. Cool to room temperature.

Makes one 9" (23 cm) pie, 8 servings

# APPLE-CRANBERRY PIE

*A fabulous fall and winter dessert that you can make a day ahead. Its lightly sweetened crisp crust marries well with the sweet, tart filling and buttery streusel topping. Pie lovers, this is one of the best pies you'll ever taste!*

**Pastry:**

| | |
|---|---|
| 1¹/₂ cups / 375 mL | unbleached flour |
| 2 tbsp / 30 mL | granulated sugar |
| ¹/₂ tsp / 2 mL | salt |
| ¹/₂ cup / 125 mL | cold unsalted butter, cubed |
| 1 | large egg yolk |
| 1 tbsp / 15 mL | cream OR milk |
| ¹/₄ cup / 60 mL | walnuts OR pecans, toasted and crushed* |

**Apple-Cranberry Filling:**

| | |
|---|---|
| 2 cups / 500 mL | cranberries, fresh or frozen, coarsely chopped |
| 3 | apples, peeled, cored, halved and thinly sliced |
| 2 tbsp / 30 mL | Grand Marnier |
| | grated zest of 1 orange |
| | juice of ¹/₂ orange |
| ²/₃ cup / 150 mL | granulated sugar |
| 1 tbsp / 15 mL | unbleached flour |
| ¹/₄ tsp / 1 mL | ground cinnamon |

**Streusel Topping:**

| | |
|---|---|
| ¹/₃ cup / 75 mL | unbleached flour |
| ¹/₄ cup / 60 mL | brown sugar |
| ¹/₄ tsp / 1 mL | ground cinnamon |
| 2 tbsp / 30 mL | unsalted butter, melted |

# APPLE-CRANBERRY PIE (CONTINUED)

Preheat oven to 350°F (175°C).

*To make the pastry*, combine flour, sugar and salt in a medium bowl. Cut butter into flour mixture with a pastry cutter until mixture resembles coarse crumbs. Alternatively, blend in a food processor. Work in egg yolk, cream and walnuts until evenly dispersed. Dough will be crumbly.

Press dough firmly and evenly against bottom and up sides of an ungreased 12" (30 cm) fluted tart pan with a removable bottom. Bake 15 minutes. Transfer to wire rack.

To *make the filling*, combine all filling ingredients in a large bowl. Spoon filling evenly into hot crust, pressing down to fill in the air pockets.

*To make the streusel topping*, combine all ingredients until crumbly; then sprinkle over filling.

Bake assembled pie 1 hour to 1 hour 15 minutes, or until fruit is tender and has released its juices. If crust browns too quickly, loosely cover pie with aluminum foil during baking. Let pie cool completely before serving.

Makes 10 to 12 servings

* Place toasted walnuts in a small plastic bag and crush with a rolling pin.

*Unsalted butter has a sweet, delicate flavor. Some recipes use the term "sweet" butter instead of unsalted butter. Salt acts as a preservative, so unsalted butter may be kept, refrigerated, for up to 3 months and salted butter up to 5 months. Wrap butter in foil to protect it from light and air – if butter oxidizes it develops a stale flavor.*

# LEMON TART

*We all have our favorite desserts and this delicious tart with its tangy filling and crisp buttery crust is one of my favorite desserts.*

**Almond Crust:**

| | |
|---|---|
| 1 cup / 250 mL | unbleached flour |
| 1/2 cup / 125 mL | cold salted butter, cut into small cubes |
| 2 tbsp / 30 mL | chopped or sliced almonds |

**Lemon Filling:**

| | |
|---|---|
| 3 | large eggs |
| 3/4 cup / 175 mL | granulated sugar |
| | grated zest of 1 lemon |
| 1/2 cup / 125 mL | fresh lemon juice |
| 1/4 cup / 60 mL | plain yogurt |

Preheat oven to 350°F (180°C).

*To prepare the crust*, place flour in a medium bowl. Cut butter into flour with a pastry cutter until mixture resembles coarse crumbs. Mix in almonds. Press dough evenly against bottom and 2/3 of the way up the side of an ungreased 9" (23 cm) pie plate.

Bake 18 minutes.

*To prepare the lemon filling*, whisk eggs and sugar together in a medium bowl. Add lemon zest, juice and yogurt and whisk until smooth. Gently pour lemon mixture into hot crust.

Bake 20 to 22 minutes, or until crust is golden and filling is set. Cool on wire rack. Just before serving, dust with icing (confectioner's) sugar, if desired.

Makes 6 to 8 servings

# BANANA, CHOCOLATE AND ORANGE TART

*Seductively simple, this puff pastry tart looks impressive and tastes as if you had spent hours in the kitchen.*

| | |
|---|---|
| 10 x 10" / 25 x 25 cm | prerolled sheet frozen puff pastry, thawed but cold |
| 2 tsp / 10 mL | butter, melted |
| 1 | seedless orange, peeled and sliced crosswise into thin rounds |
| 1 | banana, peeled and sliced |
| 1 tbsp / 15 mL | granulated sugar |
| 1 oz / 30 g | good-quality semisweet chocolate, chopped |

Preheat oven to 350°F (180°C).

Place pastry on a parchment-lined baking sheet; prick with a fork.

Brush pastry with butter. Arrange orange and banana slices on pastry, leaving a 1" (2.5 cm) border. Sprinkle with sugar and chocolate.

Bake 25 to 30 minutes, or until pastry is puffed and golden.

Makes 4 servings

# RED CURRANT MERINGUE TART

*Tangy red currants enveloped in a lightly sweetened almond meringue and baked in a crisp, shortbread-like crust. Very pleasurable, indeed!*

9" / 23 cm              Almond Crust, page 188, OR regular store-bought crust

**Red Currant Meringue Filling:**

| | |
|---|---|
| 1¼ cups / 300 mL | red currants |
| 3 | egg whites |
| ¼ tsp / 1 mL | cream of tartar |
| ½ cup / 125 mL | granulated sugar |
| ¼ cup / 60 mL | ground almonds |
| 1 tsp / 5 mL | cornstarch |

Bake pie crust in preheated 350°F (180°C) oven for 10 minutes.

*To prepare the filling*, place red currants in a large bowl.

In a small bowl, beat egg whites, cream of tartar and sugar until stiff. Beat in almonds and cornstarch. Pour over red currants and, using a wooden spoon, gently stir to coat the berries. Pour filling into hot crust.

Bake 30 to 40 minutes, or until filling is bubbly and crust is golden. Cool on a wire rack. Serve with a dollop of whipped cream, if desired.

Makes 6 to 8 servings

## DESSERTS

# CINNAMON TWISTS

*Feel like having something sweet with your afternoon tea or coffee? These rich-tasting lightly sweetened little pastries take 30 minutes to make, including baking time, and they are simply delicious.*

| | |
|---|---|
| 10 x 10" / 25 x 25 cm | prerolled sheet frozen puff pastry, thawed but cold |
| 2 tbsp / 30 mL | melted butter |
| | sprinkles of granulated sugar, cinnamon and sesame seeds |

Preheat oven to 425°F (220°C). Line a baking sheet with parchment paper.

Unroll dough. Place on a lightly floured surface and brush half with half of butter. Sprinkle liberally with sugar, cinnamon and sesame seeds. Fold remaining half sheet over filling. Gently roll out to a 12 x 18" (30 x 45 cm) rectangle. Brush with remaining melted butter and sprinkle with sugar and cinnamon.

Using a zigzag pastry cutter, cut crosswise into 20 to 24 strips. Twist strips individually with the coated side facing out. Place on baking sheet 1/2" (1.3 cm) apart. Sprinkle twists with sesame seeds.

Bake about 15 minutes, or until lightly browned. Serve warm or at room temperature. Best when eaten same day.

Makes 20 to 24 twists

# WHOOPIE PIES

*The traditional Whoopie Pie, whose origins can be traced back 50 years or more to Pennsylvania Dutch country, is an unsophisticated chocolate "sandwich cake," roughly the size of a doughnut and filled with a sweet gooey cream. For me, it's a "little taste of heaven," more pleasurable than the fanciest chocolate cake.*

| | |
|---|---|
| 2/3 cup / 150 mL | unsweetened cocoa |
| 1 tsp / 5 mL | baking soda |
| 3/4 cup / 175 mL | hot water |
| 3/4 cup / 175 mL | unsalted butter, softened |
| 1 cup / 250 mL | granulated sugar |
| 1 | egg |
| 2 tsp / 10 mL | vanilla extract |
| 1/2 cup / 125 mL | plain yogurt |
| 2 cups / 500 mL | unbleached flour |
| 1 tsp / 5 mL | baking powder |
| pinch | salt |

**Creamy Filling:**

| | |
|---|---|
| 1 cup / 250 mL | whipping cream |
| 1 cup / 250 mL | marshmallow cream |

Preheat oven to 350°F (180°C). Line a baking sheet with parchment paper.

Pour cocoa and baking soda into a medium bowl. Whisk in hot water until smooth. Set aside.

Using a fork or electric mixer, cream butter and sugar in a large bowl. Gradually add egg, vanilla, yogurt and cocoa mixture; beat until smooth. Gradually fold in flour, baking powder and salt to form a thick batter.

Scoop heaping tablespoonfuls (22 mL) of batter onto baking sheet, leaving about 2" (5 cm) between them. Using a greased knife, shape into circles and flatten slightly to measure 2" (5 cm) across.

Bake about 12 minutes per batch, or until cakes spring back when lightly pressed. Cool completely on rack before assembling "pies."

**To make the filling**, beat whipping cream until stiff. Add marshmallow cream and beat just enough to mix evenly.

**To assemble the "pies,"** place a heaping tablespoon (22 mL) of filling in center of flat sides of cakes. Top with remaining cakes, flat side down, pressing gently until the filling hits the edge.

Makes 14 to 16 Whoopie Pies

# CHOCOLATE MACADAMIA NUT BROWNIES

*All the chocoholics I know love these melt-in-the-mouth brownies. Moist centers with rich-tasting Chocolate Frosting.*

| | |
|---|---|
| ½ cup / 125 mL | butter, softened |
| 1½ cups / 375 mL | sugar |
| 2 | eggs |
| 1 cup / 250 mL | plain yogurt |
| 1 tsp / 5 mL | vanilla extract |
| 1 cup / 250 mL | unbleached flour |
| ¾ cup / 175 mL | unsweetened cocoa |
| ¾ tsp / 3 mL | baking powder |
| ½ tsp / 2 mL | salt |
| 1 cup / 250 mL | chopped macadamia nuts |

Preheat oven to 350°F (180°C).

With electric mixer, beat butter and sugar until smooth. Beat in eggs, yogurt and vanilla. Gradually mix in flour, cocoa, baking powder and salt. When smooth, fold in nuts.

Spread batter evenly in a lightly greased 9 x 13" (23 x 33 cm) baking dish. Bake about 30 minutes or until a toothpick inserted in center comes out clean. Let cool in pan on wire rack.

Spread frosting over cooled brownies. Let set, then cut into squares.

# CHOCOLATE FROSTING

| | |
|---|---|
| ¼ cup / 60 mL | boiling water |
| ¼ cup / 60 mL | unsweetened cocoa |
| 1 tsp / 5 mL | instant coffee granules |
| ¾ cup / 175 mL | butter, softened |
| 2 cups / 500 mL | icing (confectioner's) sugar |
| ½ tsp / 2 mL | vanilla extract |

In a medium bowl, stir boiling water into cocoa until smooth. Add remaining ingredients, stirring until thick and creamy.

# BUTTERSCOTCH CRUNCH

*I had my first taste of this addictively yummy candy treat when my partner Chuck's sister, Annabelle Goodman, made it for us a few months ago. She shared the recipe with me and I've since made it several times, always to rave reviews. It rivals the best commercial version of this nutty butterscotch confection, yet can be so quickly and simply made in your own kitchen.*

| | |
|---|---|
| 1/2 cup / 125 mL | EACH, butter, honey, granulated sugar, whole almonds, sliced almonds and pecan halves |
| 3 cups / 750 mL | broken matzah OR water crackers |

Combine butter, honey and sugar in a large microwavable bowl. Microwave on high for 5 minutes, stopping to stir once or twice. Add nuts and matzah, stirring to coat. Microwave 2 minutes; stir and microwave 1 to 2 minutes longer, or until lightly browned.

Spread mixture in a single layer on a parchment-lined baking sheet. Cool slightly. Wet your hands with cold water and press mixture to flatten. Let cool to room temperature, then freeze until firm and brittle, at least 2 hours. Break into pieces and store in an airtight container in the refrigerator up to 1 week or in the freezer up to 1 month.

Makes about 4 cups (1 L)

# CHOCOLATE AND ORANGE SOFT BISCOTTI

*These light-tasting soft-textured biscotti are a hit whenever I make them for family and friends. They look like you've slaved over them for hours when, in actual fact, you've only spent 20 minutes getting them ready for the oven.*

*Use good-quality chocolate and the juice and zest of fresh oranges, if possible. Biscotti with a cup of coffee ... one of life's simple pleasures.*

| | |
|---|---|
| 3/4 cup / 175 mL | butter OR margarine, softened |
| 1 cup / 250 mL | granulated sugar |
| | grated zest of 2 oranges |
| 1/4 cup / 60 mL | orange juice |
| 2 | eggs |
| 2 1/2 cups / 625 mL | unbleached flour |
| 1 tsp / 5 mL | baking powder |
| 1/3 cup / 75 mL | semisweet chocolate, coarsely chopped |
| 1/3 cup / 75 mL | milk chocolate, coarsely chopped |
| | granulated sugar and ground cinnamon, for sprinkling |

Preheat oven to 350°F (180°C).

In a medium bowl, using an electric mixer, beat together butter, sugar, orange zest, juice and eggs. Gradually stir in flour and baking powder to form a smooth firm dough. Work in chocolate.

Divide dough into 4 equal portions. Sprinkle work surface with flour and shape each portion into a 12" (30 cm) roll. Place rolls 2" (5 cm) apart on a parchment-lined cookie sheet. Flatten rolls slightly and sprinkle with sugar and cinnamon.

Bake for 13 to 15 minutes, or until edges start to brown. Remove from oven. While still warm, cut rolls diagonally into 1 1/2" (4 cm) strips, about 12 strips per roll. Place on wire rack to cool before storing in cookie tins.

Makes about 4 dozen biscotti

# COCONUT AND OATMEAL CRISPS

*Thin, crisp, light-tasting cookies. Perfect with afternoon tea.*

| | |
|---|---|
| 1/2 cup / 125 mL | unsalted butter, softened |
| 1/2 cup / 125 mL | granulated sugar |
| pinch | salt |
| 3/4 cup / 175 mL | unbleached flour |
| 1/2 cup / 125 mL | rolled oats |
| 1 3/4 cups / 425 mL | sweetened shredded coconut |

In a large bowl, cream butter, sugar and salt together until smooth. Gradually mix in flour, oats and coconut to form a firm dough. Pat into a 3 x 6" (8 x 15 cm) rectangular log. Wrap in foil and freeze about 30 minutes.

Preheat oven to 350°F (180°C).

With a sharp serrated knife, cut log crosswise into 24, 1/4" (6 mm) slices. Arrange slices on parchment-lined baking sheets, 1" (2.5 cm) apart. Bake 20 to 25 minutes, until golden. Cool on wire rack.

Makes about 24 cookies

# OAT, RAISIN AND FLAXSEED COOKIES

*Crisp on the outside, moist and chewy on the inside, these delicately orange-flavored, fibre-rich cookies are a wholesome treat.*

| | |
|---|---|
| 1 tbsp / 15 mL | flaxseeds |
| 2 tbsp / 30 mL | water |
| 1/2 cup / 125 mL | butter OR margarine, softened |
| 3/4 cup / 175 mL | packed brown sugar |
| 1/2 cup / 125 mL | granulated sugar |
| 1/4 cup / 60 mL | milk |
| 1 | large egg |
| | grated zest of 1 orange |
| 1 cup / 250 mL | unbleached flour |
| 1/2 tsp / 2 mL | baking soda |
| 2 cups / 500 mL | rolled oats |
| 1/2 cup / 125 mL | raisins |

# OAT, RAISIN AND FLAXSEED COOKIES (CONTINUED)

In a small bowl, combine flaxseeds with water. Cover; soak 2 hours to overnight.

Preheat oven to 350°F (180°C). Line cookie sheets with parchment paper.

In a medium bowl, beat together butter, sugars, milk and egg until light and fluffy. Stir in flaxseeds, orange zest, flour, baking soda, oats and raisins.

Drop dough by small spoonfuls onto cookie sheets. Bake in middle of oven for 12 to 14 minutes, or until golden. Cool on wire rack.

Makes 40 to 48 cookies

# CHOCOLATE NUGGET COOKIES

*Intensely chocolatey, with soft centers, these delectable flourless cookies will satisfy every chocolate lover's craving.*

| | |
|---|---|
| 8 oz / 250 g | good-quality semisweet dark chocolate, coarsely chopped |
| 3 tbsp / 45 mL | butter, coarsely chopped |
| 2 | eggs |
| 1/3 cup / 75 mL | granulated sugar |
| 1/2 cup / 125 mL | ground almonds |
| 1/4 cup / 60 mL | finely chopped almonds |
| 2 tbsp / 30 mL | rolled oats |
| | granulated sugar for rolling |

In a saucepan over low heat, melt chocolate and butter, stirring constantly to avoid burning. Remove from heat. Cool to room temperature.

In a small bowl, beat eggs and sugar together. Stir into chocolate mixture. Fold in remaining ingredients, cover and refrigerate 4 hours to overnight.

Preheat oven to 325°F (160°C).

Using a melon baller or teaspoon, shape dough into 1" (2.5 cm) balls. Roll in sugar and place on parchment-lined sheets, 2" (5 cm) apart. Bake 12 minutes.

Makes 30 to 34 cookies

*Pictured on page 191.*

# ALMOND BUTTER CHOCOLATE CHIP COOKIES

*These are melt-in-your-mouth treats.*

| | |
|---|---|
| ¹/₂ cup / 125 mL | salted butter, softened |
| 1 cup / 250 mL | brown sugar, packed |
| 1 | large egg |
| ¹/₂ cup / 125 mL | almond butter* |
| 1¹/₂ cups / 375 mL | unbleached flour |
| 1 tsp / 5 mL | baking soda |
| ¹/₂ cup / 125 mL | slivered almonds |
| ¹/₂ cup / 125 mL | chocolate chips |
| 1 tbsp / 15 mL | sugar |

Preheat oven to 375°F (190°C).

Cream butter and sugar in a medium bowl. Beat in egg and almond butter. Gradually stir in flour, baking soda, almonds and chocolate chips.

Drop by heaping teaspoonfuls (7 mL) on parchment-lined baking sheets, leaving room for expansion. Dip fork into sugar and slightly flatten cookies.

Bake about 10 minutes, or until cookies start to brown around the edges. Cool on wire rack.

Makes about 36 cookies

* Almond butter is available at health and specialty food stores and at many supermarkets. For **Peanut Butter Chocolate Chip Cookies**, use smooth peanut butter and substitute chopped peanuts for the almonds.

# CHOCOLATE CHUNK SHORTBREAD COOKIES

*When you offer these buttery, chocolatey cookies to guests, they'll want seconds!*

| | |
|---|---|
| 2 cups / 500 mL | butter, softened |
| 1 cup / 250 mL | fruit OR icing (confectioner's) sugar |
| 3 cups / 750 mL | unbleached flour |
| ³/₄ cup / 175 mL | rice flour |
| 12 oz / 340 g | good-quality semisweet dark OR milk chocolate, melted and cooled |

# CHOCOLATE CHUNK SHORTBREAD COOKIES
### (CONTINUED)

In a large bowl, beat butter and sugar until smooth. Mix in flours and chocolate, kneading until dough sticks together, forming a ball. Cut dough in half and shape into two, 6" (15 cm) long logs. Wrap each log tightly in foil and refrigerate 2 hours to overnight.

Preheat oven to 325°F (160°C). Cut each log into $1/4$" (6 mm) thick slices. Place on parchment-lined cookie sheets about 1" (2.5 cm) apart.

Bake 12 to 14 minutes, or until lightly browned around the edges. Let cool 1 minute, then, with spatula, transfer cookies to wire rack. Store in airtight container up to 2 weeks.

Makes about 6 dozen cookies

# CRANBERRY AND MACADAMIA NUT SHORTBREAD COOKIES

*The perfect Christmas cookie — flaky, crunchy, not too sweet.*

| | |
|---|---|
| 1 cup / 250 mL | unsalted butter, softened |
| $1/4$ cup / 60 mL | granulated sugar |
| $1/4$ cup / 60 mL | icing (confectioner's) sugar |
| $1^3/4$ cups / 425 mL | unbleached flour |
| pinch | salt |
| $1/2$ cup / 125 mL | coarsely chopped macadamia nuts |
| $1/2$ cup / 125 mL | dried cranberries |

In a large bowl, beat butter and sugars until smooth. Mix in flour and salt until mixture is crumbly. Using your hands, work in nuts and cranberries and shape dough into two 9" (23 cm) logs. Wrap in foil and refrigerate 1 hour to overnight.

Preheat oven to 300°F (150°C). Line 2 cookie sheets with parchment paper.

With a sharp knife, cut each log into 18 to 20 slices. Place on cookie sheets 1" (2.5 cm) apart.

Bake about 20 minutes, or until golden. Cool on wire rack. Store in an airtight container for up to 2 weeks.

Makes about 40 cookies

*Pictured on page 191.*

# CHOCOLATE NUT AND FRUIT CLUSTERS

*It's easy to please with these no-bake fudge-like clusters of almonds, coconut, oats, dried apricots and cranberries. Wholesome and delicious!*

| | |
|---|---|
| 1³/4 cups / 425 mL | granulated sugar |
| 1/2 cup / 125 mL | milk |
| 1/4 cup / 60 mL | cocoa powder |
| 1/4 cup / 60 mL | butter |
| 1 cup / 250 mL | sweetened flaked coconut |
| 1 cup / 250 mL | large-flake oats |
| 1/2 cup / 125 mL | chopped dried apricots |
| 1/2 cup / 125 mL | dried cranberries |
| 1/2 cup / 125 mL | slivered almonds |

Line 2 large baking sheets with waxed or parchment paper.

In a medium saucepan, combine sugar, milk, cocoa and butter; bring to a boil over high heat while stirring. Reduce heat to low and simmer, uncovered, for 2 to 3 minutes. Remove from heat and fold in remaining ingredients. Let cool about 8 minutes.

Drop mixture by heaping tablespoonfuls (22 mL) onto a parchment-lined baking sheet. Let chocolate clusters set for about 30 minutes, then transfer them to an airtight container. Refrigerate until ready to serve, up to 1 week.

Makes about 40 cookies

# INDEX

# SHARE *PLEASURES* WITH A FRIEND

Order *Pleasures* at $22.95 per book plus $4.00 (total order) for postage and handling.

*Pleasures Pure & Simple* _____ x $22.95 = $ _____

*Tofu Mania* _____ x $12.95 = $ _____

Postage and handling _____ = $ _____4.00_____

Subtotal _____ = $ _____

In Canada add 6% GST _____(Subtotal x .06) = $ _____

Total enclosed_____ = $ _____

U.S. and international orders payable in U.S. funds. U.S. shipping $5.00.
Price is subject to change

NAME  _____

STREET _____

CITY_____ PROV./STATE_____

COUNTRY _____ POSTAL CODE/ZIP _____

Please make cheque or money order payable to:

> Brita Housez
> 3 Evangelista Court
> St. Catharines, Ontario
> Canada  L2N 7C3
> FAX: 905-934-6084

For fundraising or volume purchases, contact Brita Housez.

Please allow 3-4 weeks for delivery.

# OTHER BOOKS BY BRITA HOUSEZ

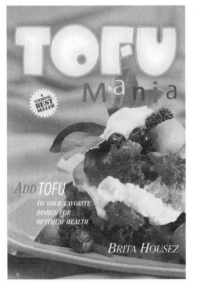

## TOFU MANIA *– add TOFU to your favorite dishes for optimum health*

Tofu demystified – add protein, calcium, vitamins, iron and natural estrogens to your diet while reducing cholesterol, fats and calories. Add DELICIOUS to describe the recipes in *Tofu Mania*. Sound unbelievable? It's true! Tofu is substituted for PART of the fat in your favorite dishes. Its mainstream popularity is due to scientific studies which conclude that tofu, and other soy foods, can help treat or prevent many diseases.

Retail $12.95        6" x 9"
120 pages       5 color photographs
ISBN 1-894022-21-1       perfect bound

## The soy dessert & baking book
*– add SOY – and NUTRITION – to your favorite cakes, cookies, pies, tarts, muffins, quick breads, puddings and other desserts*

Learn how to make even the most decadent treats healthful. All of the yummy sweets are chock full of cholesterol-free soy. All are satisfying, delicious, and perfect for the health-conscious eater. Finally, you can have your cake and eat it, too!

Retail $25.95        7" x 9¼"
214 pages       5 color photographs
ISBN 1-56924-589-4       perfect bound